T
Survival Guide

An A–Z guide to getting the Christian life sorted

Nick Harding

kevin mayhew

kevin mayhew

First published in Great Britain in 2008 by Kevin Mayhew Ltd
Buxhall, Stowmarket, Suffolk IP14 3BW
Tel: +44 (0) 1449 737978 Fax: +44 (0) 1449 737834
E-mail: info@kevinmayhewltd.com

www.kevinmayhew.com

9 8 7 6 5 4 3 2 1 0

ISBN 978 1 84867 108 9
Catalogue No. 1501146

Cover design by Rob Mortonson
Edited by Katherine Laidler
Typeset by Dave Cullen

Printed and bound in Great Britain

Introduction

If you are male, in your teens and struggling with some of the things you see in the mirror, then this book could be just right for you!

Being a teenage boy is not easy. There are many issues about growing up, physical and emotional changes, family relationships, sex and love which fill the mind with confusion. In addition, challenges like making decisions about careers and exams, and the whole area of faith and belief just add to the pressure.

So here's a book with lots of questions and hopefully a few answers too! We look at some of the key issues which teenage young men face and give some solid, honest advice. Now, as you'll see in a page or two, whether you take the advice is up to you . . . but dare you ignore it? I hope you find it really helpful.

Nick Harding

Aa

Abilities

see also Leadership

We've all got abilities and skills that make us different from our best mates or peers. Some people are really good at sports, others are scientific, others enjoy reading. If you're not sure what abilities you've got, sit down and make a list – you might be pleasantly surprised! There are practical engineers and mechanics, and artistic painters and writers. Varied abilities make our varied world – it would be really boring if everyone could do the same things the same way to the same standard.

You may be jealous of the abilities others have, or feel that you don't have the abilities you need. But the great thing about our abilities is that they're given to us by God, and no one can take them away. God didn't make a mistake giving you the abilities you've got, but he does hope you will use them!

Abuse

Abuse comes in a number of forms, and if you have suffered abuse, you probably know about them already. There are four main forms of abuse: sexual abuse, physical abuse, emotional abuse and abuse through neglect. Young people are usually abused by people who are older than them and in some form of authority over them.

Abuse is much more in the open than it used to be, but it's hard to say whether more teenagers are abused now than used to be the case. A very small minority of young people are abused in church settings by leaders, or are abused by their peers.

If you have experienced abuse, you may feel that it was your fault or that you are now of less value. God doesn't see it like that. He hates the pain that you have felt and he wants to heal the feelings and memories you have. Being a boy doesn't mean you are responsible and should have stood up for yourself. It is never right for anyone to be abused by someone else. If you are treated badly or touched in a way that makes you feel uncomfortable, don't keep it a secret, but tell an adult you trust.

Addiction

see also Balance, Booze, Cigarettes, Drugs, Eating Disorders, Solvents

Addiction is not all about drugs! Many people get addicted to all sorts of things. You may know people who are addicted to coffee. You know the sort – people who grab the coffee jar like it's the greatest treasure in the world and they have to have it right now! Some people even get addicted to not eating or to losing weight. Other people develop an addiction to a cola drink, to smoking, to drugs of various kinds, to computer games, to sports . . . in fact, to just about anything.

Addiction to anything is not healthy. God designed us to make the most of everything that we can find in life. If we get addicted to one particular thing, we are going to miss out on the other things on offer. And it is obvious that some addictions mess us up mentally and physically too. So don't get addicted; just enjoy what you know is good and steer clear of the other rubbish.

Adolescence

This is the time of your life when you change from being a boy to being a man. Your hormones change and can affect your moods, your testosterone makes you get serious about girls, and you start to masturbate and get erections. The beginning of adolescence is called puberty, and the whole changing time can start at different ages for different guys, and take quite a few years to go through.

Adolescence is not an easy time and it can be really confusing. But however tough it is for you, it is making you into a man and the change is for the better. God's time is the right time, and you'll survive!

Advice

There's a lot of it about! This book is full of it, and so are friends, parents, brothers and sisters, TV programmes, magazines, internet chat sites and so on. There are counsellors who are keen to listen to problems and offer advice, and people at church who would be more than willing to share their wisdom with you.

Advice always pushes a point of view. For instance, a computer salesman would probably advise you to buy the most expensive model. Your teachers may advise you to spend all your spare time doing homework and revising. This book gives advice from a Christian point of view, showing what God thinks about situations.

Whatever advice you are offered, it's up to you whether you take the advice or not. Read it, listen to it and think it through. If it makes sense to you and you feel that it's the best (if not necessarily the most enjoyable) way, then follow the advice. The choice is yours!

Aggression

You know that the world is not always as safe as it should be. Teenage lads can be the victims of hate crimes, racism or aggression for no particular reason at all. Many people in society are only really concerned about what they want and can be violent and aggressive in order to get what they want. This is a bad state and not how God wanted it to be.

It must make him feel really sad to see young people using knives and guns against each other.

As you grow up, there will be times when things go wrong, when you see injustice or when something happens that makes you really angry. It's really important to remain calm and remember what Jesus says about peace, forgiveness and calm.

AIDS

see also Love, Sex

You will know about this already. You should also know that the only way you can catch the HIV virus is through body fluids. You can't catch it by using a loo seat, touching clothes, kissing or hugging.

AIDS is still a serious world illness passed on through sexual activity, blood, or using dirty needles in drug-taking. It is not God's intentional judgement on a world that ignores him, but it is a result of a world that doesn't follow God's advice.

'Safe' sex – using a condom – is promoted as the best way to avoid the HIV virus and AIDS. But condoms can go wrong, and some stats suggest that 30% fail when used by young people. The only really safe way to avoid it is to keep sex to permanent relationships, God's ideal being marriage.

Arguments

see also Home Life, Hormones

Have a think: when did you last have a really big argument? Most of us have arguments from time to time, and they're not always bad things. Through arguments you are able to develop your own point of view and challenge what others think. Through arguments you can let off steam and get rid of some deep anger and frustration. Even the disciples of Jesus had arguments, mostly about who Jesus liked best . . . wow! It's likely that you will be in the mood to argue more than you used to be as you move from being a boy to a man.

But arguments have a downside. During arguments you can say things you don't mean and cause hurt. You can fall out with family members and friends. Most of all, you can argue something that everyone knows is wrong, and you end up looking like a right idiot! So be cool – think before you open your mouth!

Armed Forces

see also Careers, War, Work

Most boys have imagined being a brave fighter in the army, a skilled pilot or a sailor hero. But now it's time for the truth: there's no glamour in being in the armed forces! Apart from the reality of having to be available to kill others if ordered to, there's a lot of hard work involved in getting fit enough before you apply to join, tests and exams before recruitment, and then a long period of recruit training. And most of the jobs available in the armed forces don't involve charging through forests with guns or jumping out of aeroplanes.

The Armed Forces can provide good careers for young men (and women too!) who are really committed to it. Be open to what God wants you to do when you're older, and allow him to change your mind if he wants to.

Bb

Bad News

see also Death

Bad news can really affect teenagers, partly because the changes you're going through affect the way you think and respond to situations, and partly because you are now able to understand things as an adult as well as a child. Life isn't always easy, and it could be that over the next few years you may hear bad news about the death of a good friend or a close family member, your father may lose his job, or your mother may become ill. Bad news makes you ask fundamental questions like 'Why does this happen?' and 'How are we going to cope?'

Bad news is part of what we all have to face, but it's not to be faced on your own. When you have bad news, it's time to make the most of the people around you by talking to your friends, seeing your youth leader, and discussing how you feel with your church leader. God seems to be a long way away when bad news comes through, but really he never moves away and cares deeply for the pain you are going through.

Balance

see also Addiction

This is such a boring, adult word! You may have a parent at home who talks to you about getting a bit of balance in your life. Your teachers may have gone on about a balanced attitude towards schoolwork, homework and leisure activities.

Balance is all about getting the level of something right. You'd go mad if you spent all your time doing just one thing, and your life would become unbalanced. To even things up you need to get the balance right.

Let's think, for instance, about how you spend your time. If you use up all your time on the internet, you will not have the balance of real friendships and relationships in your life. If you spend all your time at church, you'll forget what the real world is like. If you spend all your time thinking about girls, you'll lose the plot. And if you spend all your time in your room doing homework, you'll probably become a boring swot!

Try this: make a list of all the things you do in a week and how much time you devote to each thing. If there's one thing (apart from sleep and school) which has taken over, get the balance right – and get a life!

Baptism

see also Church, Confirmation

You may have been baptised or christened as a baby or child – many people are. But some churches believe baptism is a good thing for a teenager or adult to go through once they are old enough to know what it means to love God and want to be a follower of Jesus.

To be baptised as a teenager you'll need to be brave, seriously committed to God and determined to live differently. You could use the service as a chance to invite your friends along, in the same way as a Confirmation service. It is a great thing to do if that's your church tradition and it can really strengthen your faith.

Bedrooms

see also Home Life

Rubbish tips and school cloakrooms are usually about as tidy as boys' bedrooms!

Your bedroom is your space, where you can do your own thing and keep your belongings. It's somewhere to go to when you want some time on your own, when you've had a row, when you want to pray or think, or when you want to do something in private. Your bedroom has your smell, your colours, and your dirty pants under the bed! You probably hate having your space invaded by a mother, a Hoover or a brother!

If you share your room, it's hard, as you know! Then you have to think more carefully about the state of your room and how much of the space you want for yourself. You may have to work out ground rules with the person you share with and agree to consider each other.

If you want more control of your own space and don't want it invaded, tidied and cleaned, then make a deal. Promise that you'll keep it reasonably tidy yourself, and that in return your parents shouldn't march in and examine your property. But remember – this'll only work if you keep your part of the bargain!

Bible

see also God, Jesus

If you think the Bible is a dusty old book full of improbable stories and irrelevant writings, then you've got a lot to learn! There is no other book with such energy, such wisdom and such sound advice. It's not for reading from front to back, and it's best to read it with help from notes and with the help of others.

The Bible takes us to the heart of what God is all about. It shows a loving God who made the world and led his people despite their mistakes. It shows the Son of God coming to earth as a poor baby, being born in a dump and dying for every one of us. And it gives advice for everyone on just about every problem we may face.

Don't ignore the Bible, because it's got far more to teach you than this book or any other book, film, website or story! Get some Bible notes to help you, talk to an adult about understanding it more, and read it.

Boasting

see also Abilities, Good News, Popularity

We all like to show off sometimes. Boasting is part of each of us trying to prove that we are different and better than other people. We may boast about our home or family, about our possessions, experiences or abilities. But most boasting isn't true, and most people don't believe boasters.

God turns this attitude upside-down. He advises everyone to be humble, which means being quiet about our abilities and considering others. We will get much more respect if we go about life in an ordinary way rather than shouting, 'Look at me – aren't I great!' all the time!

Booze

see also Addiction, Balance

Drink, alcohol, grog! Like many other things, alcoholic drinks are targeted and advertised at you. You are meant to be cool and attractive if you drink, and it's supposed to show that you are an adult. Suddenly you are supposed to become mature, be 'one of the lads' and draw the attention of the best girls around.

But what is the reality of having alcohol, especially before you are a fully grown adult? You're likely to feel or even be sick, you will feel dehydrated, you will lose your power of judgement, and your emotions will get all confused. You could find yourself declaring undying love to your best friend and trying to snog him, or walking wildly out into the road in front of a bus! And then there's the feeling that a drill is hammering your head and that you've died and gone to hell in the morning. And if you've bought a drink and you're under 18, you've broken the law!

Booze is no joke. It's addictive, it makes you behave like an idiot, and it is a poison. Teenagers drink an alarming amount of alcohol and are putting their future health at serious risk. It's now thought that more girls than boys drink excessively and dangerously. Over a longer term alcohol will do permanent and serious damage to your body and your brain. Most of all, it stops you knowing what you are doing, and that's not the way God wanted it to be.

Boredom

see also Jobs at Home, Misery, Work

'I'm bored,' says the teenager, and 'I'm bored!' thinks the adult! Boredom is a state of mind that many people suffer from as they go about their normal days with no excitement and no challenges. Rainy Sunday afternoons are the most boring times ever! The sad truth is that there are many things in life that are boring, and now's as good a time to learn it as any!

If you get bored, don't tell your parents – they'll find you something even more boring to do! Instead find a friend to see, or have a go at a new challenge. It won't change how you feel completely, but it may take away that dull ache of frustration.

Brothers

see also Sisters

They can be fantastic and they can be a nightmare! Brothers are often rivals, trying to prove that they are stronger, bigger or better than the other. So brothers fight and argue, they get each other into trouble, and they play nasty tricks. But older brothers have their uses. They may have more money to give you or buy you things. They may be big enough to be a threat for you to use against people who have a go at you. Younger brothers can be cute and therefore able to get things out of parents that you can't. They've also got toys and games which you like to mess around with but are too old to own yourself . . . like Lego!

The bottom line about brothers is that you don't get the chance to choose them and you are stuck with them, so you might as well make the most of them!

Bullying

see also Gangs

Did you know that many adults complain of being bullied at work? Bullying isn't something confined to the school playground, and it's not something anyone should put up with.

Bullies are weak people with their own problems. They misuse their power over others by threats and accusations. They are rarely on their own and need the support of other sad cowards. They target people who stand out and are different, whether that is because of what they wear, how they behave, what they believe or what they are or are not able to do.

There is no excuse for bullying and, whatever it takes, we've all got a role to play in stopping bullies getting away with it. If you are being bullied, it's best not to try to argue or fight back. Instead tell someone with authority like a teacher, church group leader or a parent, and don't let it go until it's sorted. And if you witness bullies in action on someone else, don't ignore it – get help for them.

If you want to be seen as a man rather than a boy, this is your chance to prove it – don't give bullies a chance!

Cc

Careers

see also Decisions, Work

When you were younger you may have wanted to drive Thomas the Tank Engine or work with Fireman Sam on Jupiter! Now you're having to think about the career choices that are really open to you, and what you feel you may want to do.

It is not easy to choose a career, and your choices of exam courses now does not mean you can't change your mind about your future work later. But now is the time to take as much advice as you can, spend time with people who do the job you like the look of, and pray about what God might want you to do. Don't restrict yourself to jobs that 'men' are supposed to do – there's equality these days! Make the effort to listen to what your parents have to say, even if you think they don't understand you.

Most of us have to make our choices for the future without hearing God's voice directly like Samuel did in the Bible, but God will make things clear and open the way for us if we ask him.

Cars

see also Wants

Wheels give freedom and street cred! Cars are attractive and glamorous, fast enough to keep up with the average energetic young man. You may imagine looking really cool cruising the streets in your local town.

Cars are given an image which they really don't deserve! TV programmes and magazines make them out to be some sort of gods, and people worship them by cleaning and polishing them on Sunday mornings when the rest of us are in church! Yet in reality cars are tin boxes designed to get people from A to B, lethal weapons in the wrong hands, and very expensive to run. Badly driven cars kill and injure thousands of people every year, with many more accidents being caused by the inexperienced 17-25 year-old drivers than all other ages.

Don't be too eager to get yourself a car, or at least be real about the danger, the problems, the work and the cost. And remember that God asks us to worship him, not a shiny tin box!

Certificate 18

see also TV

Most young people watch TV programmes and videos which are not made or designed for their age group. I guess you have seen horror films that have scared you lots, violence which has remained strong in your memory, and sex scenes which reveal things which you were not supposed to see until later in life.

There are good reasons why films have age warnings on them. Despite how it seems, it is not a case of adults wanting to keep secrets or be spoilsports. Decisions on 'Certificate 15' and 'Certificate 18' films are made by groups of people who understand the damage inappropriate scenes can cause in the minds of teenagers. They have to draw the line somewhere, or even very young children would be allowed to watch things that would damage them.

It may seem fun to get together and watch films that have a 'Certificate' classification which is older than you are, but do you really think it's right to do so?

Church

see also Baptism, Confirmation, Cults, Religions

Church is about people, not about the building. The first believers, who gathered after Jesus had ascended to heaven, met in small rooms and people's houses, and some churches still do. Your church may have a tower or steeple; it may be old or modern. But what really matters is what goes on for and with the people.

You may think church is boring. You may think the songs are all too old, the sermons and talks are too long, and that no one understands what it's like for you. The Bible tells us to meet together to worship God and to learn more about the way he wants us to live our lives, yet it can seem like a couple of hours of boring agony every week.

No church is perfect, because the people who make up the church make mistakes . . . like you do! If you want your church to change, it is no use leaving it, staying at home and not taking part. You can only have a part to play if you get involved, make the best of it and make your views known. Remember – whatever others in your church may think, you belong to it as much as they do.

Cigarettes

see also Addiction

When your grandparents were young, smoking was a really cool thing to do and most young people did it. No one realised the health issues that surround cigarettes. Now it's still seen by some as a really big thing to do, despite the fact that over 100,000 people a year die as a result of illnesses caused by smoking or breathing in others' smoke. Basically cigarettes are a major, slow and painful killer.

Smoking is a big waste of money and a big waste of time. It ruins clothes with the awful stench, and it's impossible to hide the smell from parents and friends, however hard you try. Many accidental fires are caused by careless use of matches and careless disposal of nub-ends. It causes others to have to walk through and breathe in a fog of fumes and tar which clings to the throat, air passages and lungs. And it's not nice to be near boys who smell like ash-trays!

If you have started smoking cigarettes, the bad news is that it's addictive and you might find it hard to get off them. You may be locked in to depending on cigarettes, always having yellow stains on your hands and in your home, always having to find money for the next packet, always knowing that each drag may be contributing to your death. But the good news is that God doesn't want you to kill yourself like this! The younger you are and the sooner you try to get off cigarettes, the easier it is, so give it a try and get help if you're struggling. It has to be worth it!

Cleanliness

see also Hair, Zits

Have you ever had your parents send you back to the bathroom to have another wash because they don't believe that you washed in the first place? They are only trying to teach you to be clean!

Cleanliness is really important for a teenage male. Spots and zits will be worse than they need be because they love settling into skin that is greasy and dirty. Hair needs more washing than normal to avoid it going really weird. And as you grow, so sweat glands become increasingly active and make you smell foul if you don't give your armpits and a few other places some attention. After-shave and deodorants between washes don't cover up nasty smells, they just add to the nastiness. And watch out for after-shave – if you use too much after shaving it will sting horribly and make you smell like a cheap perfume shop. If you keep clean, you will feel better, smell better, your clothes will last longer, and you will look better to the opposite sex!

Computer Games

see also Abilities, Balance

These provide a challenge and give users a real buzz and determination to win. They are always there ready to be used and are attractive, well-produced and very realistic.

Young men really enjoy playing computer games of all kinds. It's great fun to try to avoid the shower of meteors falling from the top of the screen or dodge the shots of the masked murderer on your tail! But even computer games have their risks if you get too into them.

Many computer games are based on violence of one kind or another. You have to be aggressive and violent to get through into the next level, 'killing' as many victims as you can as you go. This attitude is not something that is easy to leave behind as you switch off the machine, and it can linger in the brain.

Computer games are often something you do on your own. You may enjoy being shut in your room for hours on end trying to reach level ten of Grand Theft Auto, but you should be spending some of your time with others too. If you become too cut off from others, you'll find it hard to make friends, find yourself left out of groups, and struggle to relate to your family.

Like many things, playing computer games is great if you keep it under control!

Confirmation

see also Baptism, Church

If you were baptised as a child or baby, you may well have heard Confirmation mentioned in your church. Confirmation is an opportunity for young people and adults to take on for themselves the promises to trust God that were made on their behalf as babies by parents and Godparents.

Confirmation is an important step on your journey through faith. It gives you a chance to speak out and declare that you're strong enough to live as Jesus calls you and that you're a valuable part of the church. By inviting your friends you can share with them what they're missing!

If you're not sure about Confirmation, talk to a youth group leader or someone else in church who understands young people.

Cricket

see also Football, Sport

There are plenty of teenage lads who really enjoy playing, watching and analysing the game of cricket. There are complex tactics to take into consideration, as well as pure power in fast-bowling and pure skill and judgement in batting.

Cricket is not a god, and therefore we should keep it in its right place. It's good to play and follow as a hobby, but if it takes the place of your personal faith and commitment to Jesus, then it's getting too big in your life. Unless you're a world-class player, it's not likely to offer you a career, so don't let it take over now!

Crime

Up to 7 per cent of teenage boys have a criminal records in the UK, and most of the Western world has a growing problem with teenagers breaking the law. In some communities it's seen as being big or clever to do things that are antisocial and cause damage to other people's property. God wants us to respect each other and the world he made, not cause damage or pain.

Some young people do one or two minor things wrong and learn from their mistakes. But the more you get on your record, the more it will affect what you will be able to do in the future. Some jobs will not be able to accept applicants who have committed certain crimes, and most crimes that teenagers commit remain on their criminal record for life.

If you see a crime being committed, don't intervene unless you're sure you'll be safe, but do report it. If you are tempted to commit a crime, resist the temptation . . . it's just not worth it!

Cults

see also Church, Faith

A real Christian church is not a cult. With the rise of house churches, youth congregations, cell groups and Alpha courses, it's clear that Christians do not all meet in what we would call traditional churches any more. Remember – any group of believers where Jesus is the centre of worship is probably OK.

We all have to be very careful about what we're getting into. Cults have dodgy teachings and often base what they say on special writings and books other than the Bible, or reject any established and formal teachings. Cults often target young people and try to take advantage of your energy and wish to make things better. So, for instance, they may talk a lot about saving the planet and the evils of pollution. Cults may advise you to ignore or defy what your parents tell you or to go against others in authority. And cults will probably not be keen for your parents or other adults you trust to come with you and see what happens.

Let's be honest here – cults can seem very attractive and are often led by powerful and seemingly caring people. They say things which young people like to hear, and avoid answering straight questions with gentle, honest-sounding replies.

If you are drawn in to any group, make sure you have your eyes wide open. It's not strong or clever to trust your own judgement alone. If you have any doubts, don't go along, and find out more before you think about going again.

Dd

Deadlines *see also Abilities, Homework, School*

Before you read this, check that all your homework is up to date. Is it? OK then! Deadlines for handing in homework and course work are not always evil dates which are best ignored or avoided! Teachers generally try hard to give you a spread of work so that it doesn't all come along at once, and the dates and deadlines they set are there to help you get the work done without having to rush or do too much at any one time.

Most teenage boys leave work until the very last moment . . . or a little after the last moment! This gives you more free time spread out until the mad rush at the end. You may even find that you work best if there's a deadline ahead – it can help to focus the mind! But all this work is about you doing your best, not to be seen as a swot but as respect for yourself. It's not good to know that you could have done better and tried harder, that you've let yourself down. God has given you abilities, and it's like throwing them back in his face if you don't use them.

So how about trying this: get your work done as soon as you get it, and then relax knowing you've done your best. You may even have time to enjoy watching your mates panicking at the last minute!

Death

see also Bad News, Suicide

It's good to imagine that you're indestructible and you're going to live for ever. Death is seen as something to do with old people, not young and energetic ones. Yet sooner or later you will know someone who is not old and dies. Then death becomes a shock and a very real issue.

Life is about death, and death is about life! In a physical sense we will all die. Our bodies will pack up on us and our heart will no longer beat, robbing the brain of blood and closing us down. For some death comes at the end of a great deal of suffering and is seen as a relief, while for others death seems to come too quickly or too suddenly. We never know when it will come to us, and so we live our lives fully.

Death doesn't have to be the end. God promises life that lasts for ever for those who follow him and trust Jesus with their lives. We don't know quite what that eternal life will be like, although God promises it will be as good as we could possibly imagine. But no one can get it for us – it's up to us and our relationship with God.

Decisions

see also Careers

Life is full of decisions, from what clothes to wear to what career to choose. We all struggle to make decisions and often feel too big or too proud to ask others what decisions they think we should make. And we all make wrong decisions and have to suffer the consequences of doing so.

God has a role to play in all aspects of our lives. The Bible is full of people who made decisions on their own and suffered, and also those who turned to God for help and made the right choice. If you trust God, allow him to help you with the decisions you have to make – and be amazed!

Depression

see also Hormones, Misery, Suicide

Depression is much more than being a little down or feeling miserable. We might say, 'I feel depressed', but chances are we are not really depressed at all but just having a bad day. Mood swings and feelings of misery are normal as your hormones change and you move from being a boy to being a man.

Depression, not uncommon in teenage boys, is a feeling of total despair and a sense of worthlessness that lasts. Depression can be brought about by bullying or failure, or fear of exams and challenges we feel we can't face. Teenagers sometimes get depressed when they think about their future. It can also be a consequence of addiction to alcohol or drugs. Teenage boys are more likely than girls to get depressed, and also more likely to consider and attempt suicide due to depression.

Depression is a serious condition and needs treatment, initially from a doctor. It is not something that can be shaken off or beaten by positive thinking. But God cares for us all, whatever state we're in, and heals even the most serious problems. If you sometimes feel worse than being fed up, or you know someone who seems to get seriously down, don't ignore it.

Diets

see also Eating Disorders, Food

We are all on diets, because diets are simply what we feed ourselves with! Maybe we like the thought of a fast-food diet with burgers morning, noon and night. Or perhaps we are more attracted by a biscuit and crisps diet.

A lot of girls diet to lose weight, and in most cases it does no harm. Some boys have a weight problem too and have to learn to watch what they eat and be careful about it. Dieting is nothing to be ashamed of and nothing to hide – it shows that you care about your appearance and you have respect for the body God gave you. All sportsmen and women, pop stars and TV presenters have to be very careful about what they eat, otherwise they wouldn't be able to do their work properly.

Diets to lose weight are only harmful when they cut out too much food or when they become an obsession. And God doesn't think any less of you if you don't lose weight instantly or you have a binge on chips occasionally!

Divorce

see also Family, Home Life, Marriage

If you are not from a 'split' family, then it's likely that up to half of your friends are. Divorce usually comes as the result of a long period of difficulties in a marriage, and culminates in the couple splitting up and one or other moving out of the house. God didn't want it to be that way, but we live in an imperfect world full of imperfect people who make mistakes.

God would like marriages to last and families to be stable and settled, but he still loves the people involved when marriages and families go wrong.

Divorce hits all kinds of families, and Christian families are not immune from marriage difficulties. For children in the middle of a divorce, it's natural to feel that they are responsible for it all in some way and caused it to happen, but this is simply not true. It's also part of the experience to take sides, yet often both sides of a divorce have done things that have not helped the relationship to grow. If you are hurting after a divorce in your family, nothing is gained by hating your father, resenting your mother or blaming God that it happened in the first place.

God loves us all and wants to bring healing to all situations and pain. He can heal the memories and hurt felt by children, parents and friends involved. He can help people get over their experiences of divorce and look forward to their own successful marriage later in life.

Doubts

see also Questions

We've all suffered doubts. There is self-doubt about our own abilities or attractiveness, and most teenagers have doubts about their faith. In many ways it is good to have doubts because it shows that you are becoming an adult, willing to think things through for yourself and not simply accept everything that's thrown at you.

If you have doubts about Christianity, you might feel a little scared or lost, particularly if you have been brought up in a church and are from a Christian family. Suddenly it may seem that all the things you relied on may not be true after all. But if you have doubts, you are not letting God or anyone else down. It's right to ask questions and look at things from your own perspective. God doesn't call us to follow him like weak, thoughtless zombies going along with everything we're told without a second thought. He wants us to develop our own faith and trust in him, and we can only do that if we think about it and find out more about the things that raise questions in our mind.

Talk to leaders, talk to other Christians and, most of all, talk to God. He wants to know what you feel and what you think, and he will help you through.

Dreams

Dreams are weird! Scientists are fascinated by what dreams are and what they mean. In simple terms, the brain needs to sort itself out while we are asleep, and lots of images flash through. Sometimes we see these as pictures and find dreams forming into stories. They can be very real, very funny or very scary! It can also be really frustrating to remember that you had a great dream but not be able to remember what was in it!

For boys dreams can also be part of growing up. People talk of boys having 'wet dreams', which simply means that while your brain is running through its processes you wet the bed a little with semen from your penis. This can seem scary but is quite normal and nothing to be ashamed of . . . although you'd probably not want to tell your sister!

Drugs

see also Addiction

Drugs are natural or chemical substances that alter your physical or mental state. Drugs prescribed by doctors can be really helpful. Drugs kept at home like paracetamol and aspirin have a part to play in helping you if you're in pain. Drugs bought on the streets, taken on street corners or in clubs are bad news, even for the coolest of cool young men!

Drug-taking is a major problem amongst young people. Many drugs available in schools or on street corners are addictive and cumulative, meaning that the more you have, the more you need. This ties users into a permanent and very expensive reliance on them, often leading to crime in order to finance the habit.

The harm caused by drugs varies from vomiting to death, and passes through liver, brain and other organ damage, severe dehydration, mental illness and the risk of serious infections such as hepatitis and the AIDS virus, HIV. Drug users who become addicted and need to inject their drugs suffer from deep vein thrombosis, which means they struggle to walk, their blood system goes wrong, and usually they can't work.

Most drugs speed up the heart rate and give a burst of energy which is not natural and therefore causes damage. Other drugs can slow down the user's system so much that they become unable to stand and may drift into a coma. Either way it is very dangerous to mess around with the body in this way.

In all cases drugs cause the user to lose control, and they often do not know what they are doing or saying, how stupid they look, or what danger they are in. Some young people die of overdoses or of taking drugs that are mixed with scouring powder or sugar, and many others live the rest of their lives with mental and physical damage.

God doesn't want you to use such expensive, dangerous stimulants to have a good time. He made us, he knows what's best for us and he speaks the truth. Druggies are deluded and have been sold a lie.

Ee

Eating Disorders

see also Addiction, Diet, Food

There are a number of different and very complex eating disorders including anorexia nervosa and bulimia nervosa. Eating disorders usually develop in young people, both girls and, increasingly boys, when they are really worried about their body image and weight. Eating disorders can cause obsessive behaviour, severe and rapid weight loss, the failure of internal organs and, in the worst cases, death.

God made you as you are. Of course, you can improve that by looking after yourself and keeping healthy, but not by starving yourself! If you are starting to obsess about your weight and looks, get help now – and see yourself as our loving Creator God sees us.

Email

see also Computer Games, Internet, Social Networking

Modern life can be such fun! Email opens up methods of communication which are reasonably cheap and keep you in touch with friends regularly and quickly. You can exchange news, ask questions about homework, and have plenty of time for the latest gossip.

Email relationships can never replace real ones, and a name at the top of an email message cannot necessarily be trusted. There are people out there who use the internet as a means of deceiving people, drawing them in to things that are not good, or of developing wrong and unhealthy relationships. Email friendships have been known to develop between teenage boys and men who want to abuse them in some way. So be careful about who you communicate with and what you say, and keep private information like your full name and address to yourself unless you know the person you are emailing as a real person and you really trust them!

Embarrassment

see also Self-Worth

There is no one alive who could honestly say that they have never been embarrassed. We often show our embarrassment by looking away or by blushing, and it only gets worse when some clever dick says, 'Look, he's embarrassed!'

So what sort of thing embarrass teenage lads? Well, just about everything really! There are certain girls who you want to talk to but you get embarrassed when they approach. There's your family who spot you and shout 'Cooeee!' when you're hanging around with your mates. You may be embarrassed by the need to shave or the fact that you don't need to shave. You may be embarrassed by the spots on your face. You may be embarrassed by what is revealed when you go swimming or get changed for games at school. You may be embarrassed by things your mother finds in your bedroom (a good reason for tidying it yourself!). You may be embarrassed by the fact that you actually go to church and you are a Christian.

Embarrassment is all about what other people think of us. Yet if we know that God loves us (which he does), then there's nothing to be embarrassed about. Don't let others get to you; just get on and enjoy life!

Evil

see also Occult, X Files

We might picture the devil in our minds as a little man in a red costume, with a pointy tail and large fork! This image of evil makes many people think it's all a joke, when it certainly isn't.

The Bible talks about the everlasting battle between good and evil. As a result there is real evil which prompts people to do evil things to each other and behave in ways which are opposed to God's rules. Evil leads people to take interest in horoscopes and ouija boards, and gets into minds. Evil is on the news every day.

God is stronger than evil. Although there are bad things going on in the world, God is in control and when Jesus returns all evil will be wiped out. In the meantime it's best to avoid anything that may be wrong and stick to God's good plan for our lives.

Exams

see also Homework, School

There aren't many people who enjoy exams . . . but those who do are a bit sad! Seriously, exams are one of those irritants in life which have to be endured but are rarely enjoyed.

The key to coping with exams is to remember that they don't last for ever. For a while before them it makes sense to plan a proper revision timetable, to get plenty of sleep and to take exercise. Then learn things systematically and slowly, with plenty of short breaks and little treats. It doesn't help to panic and rush revision, to go for late-night cramming sessions, or to give in to the temptation that doing anything, even the washing up, offers when you should be learning stuff.

Being locked inside revising when the weather's good and your mates seem to have learned everything is not easy. But in the end it's up to you to do your best with the brains God has given you, to get the exam over, and then chill out knowing that you've proved to yourself that you can do it!

Exclusion

see also School, Teachers

School exclusions are on the rise, with more and more teenage boys in particular being sent home for a short-term, longer-term or permanent exclusion. Exclusion does not mean that the school or the teachers hate you, but it does mean that they can't do their job properly while you're there. If you're excluded, you have probably been warned about your behaviour before and have still disrupted the class too much, threatened or even caused injury to another pupil, or refused to do something you have been reasonably asked to do.

Being excluded from school is not big, and it does no one any harm but yourself. Other pupils will soon move on and forget what a big star you were for disrupting the class. The teachers will be able to get on and teach others without having to worry about what you're about to do. You will be losing out on lessons and learning which may help your future, and your parents will probably be very upset and hurt by your behaviour. So who gains? You don't, that's for sure. Take time to think about the harm you're causing, and get help from someone who will listen and talk to you about your problems at school. And remember that God doesn't hate you and wants to help you.

Ff

Faith

see also Bible, God, Jesus, Religion

Having faith is all about trusting God, that he knows what is best and that everything is in his hands. Imagine, for instance, when you were young and you held your mum or dad's hand when you crossed the road. At that point you had total faith in them and you trusted that they had your safety in mind.

Having faith in God is more than just holding on to God's hands when you're in danger. Having faith means more than just knowing the Bible stories or praying occasionally. True faith in God is about relationship with him, about giving your life to God and holding nothing back. Logically we know that God can do anything for us and only has the best for us in his plan, but when it comes to really having faith in God, it's hard to make that step, and it takes real strength and guts. Whether you have a true faith in God is a question only you can answer, but you won't know what it's like until you try!

Family *see also Brothers, Divorce, Fathers, Home Life, Mothers, Parents, Sisters*

There's no perfect model for a family, and about half young people don't have what used to be thought of as a 'normal' family life. Families may have the birth mum and dad, no dad, no mum, two dads, two mums or grandparents in charge. Whatever your family is like, there's a couple of important things to remember. Firstly, you're not responsible for the family that you're part of, and so if others don't think it's right, that's their problem and not yours. Secondly, we don't get the chance to choose everyone in our family, so you're not wrong or weird if you don't always get on with other family members.

Families in the Bible are rarely perfect, but time and time again God shows that families are important. Try to cope with yours, learn from it and, if nothing else, find out how you will run your family differently when you're much older!

Fashion *see also Peers, Shops*

Have you ever looked at those old photos of your parents? Their clothes are hilarious, their hair appalling, and as for those shoes . . . ! Fashions change so often and so rapidly that it is really hard for old fogeys like parents to keep up. Fashions say things about the wearers. Fashionable clothes say that the wearer has no individuality and has to go along with the crowd. They say that the wearer has more money than sense, and that they will be ready to splash out with more money when the next fashion comes along. Now, don't get me wrong – there's nothing wrong with looking good, but don't you think you're worth more than the clothes you are wearing and people should judge you for who you are rather than what covers up your skin? God thinks you're worth much more!

Fathers

see also Home Life, Mothers, Parents

Everyone has a different idea of what a dad is and what he should do. Some dads move away from the family home when things go wrong, and try to have contact with their children. Others move on and don't seem to want to know. Sometimes a new dad enters the family and tries to take over the fatherly role.

God's ideal for fathers is that they should provide for, protect and look after those they care for. Looking after can also mean disciplining and instructing. But fathers are also expected to show their love for their children by only giving them what is good. They have to be forgiven for hating your music, going on about 'in my day', and telling you that money doesn't grow on trees – it all goes with the territory!

Teenage boys and dads don't always get on. Some dads can feel threatened by another man growing into the family and maybe in some ways wish you were the same little boy you used to be. And you want to prove that you are a man by challenging rules and making daft threats. But stick in there because it will pass and, once you both get used to who you are, lads and dads can be a great combination.

Fear

see also Doubts, Independence

Teenage boys are supposed to be fearless and strong. But it's a fact that you have probably got more hang-ups than the girls in your class! Fears can revolve around the future, home life, failure at school, relationships. You may remember fears of spiders, the dark or monsters. Some fears can become phobias that affect the way you think and the way you live your life, and these need special attention and help.

Because the world still has an outdated view of manhood, many boys are scared to face their fears and ask people to help them through. They think that being a man, however young, means that you are not allowed to show fear of anything. But there's no point in suffering fear or being scared of something for the rest of your life just because you think you have to go through it. If you have fears that stick around and nag away at you, get someone to talk with you and pray with you about them.

Fitness

see also Diets, Food, Sport

Being fit is a good state to be in. There is a lot to be gained by taking exercise, playing games, participating in sports and being active. You may be really good at sport and a winner, or you may just take part because you know it does you good. You can also make sure you are fit by being checked out by dentists, doctors and other medical professionals. There's no doubt that it's right to keep fit.

But fitness is not only about what we do with our bodies. The Bible reminds us that we need to be fit in our minds too. We should be careful about what we watch on TV, what we read, websites we visit on the internet and what we listen to in case it's stuff that blocks our minds up with rubbish and leads our thoughts away from God. Dirty magazines, horror movies and music full of bad language don't help us keep our minds fit.

Now, if we're unfit, we might have a long way to go to get fit. But it's another of those challenges in life which are worth facing, and with God's help we can do it.

Food

see also Diets, Eating Disorders

There's plenty of it for us all to enjoy . . . in the rich developed world at least. Food is something we all take for granted. It is either something to be enjoyed and savoured as we appreciate the textures and flavours, or it is something to be thrown down as fuel before dashing off to do something else. In our country greed is a real issue, and an increasing number of young people are becoming overweight and obese through eating too much of the wrong kinds of food. Fruit and vegetables help us all get a little more balance into our diet.

Next time you are about to grab a meal and throw it down your neck, stop for a moment and ask yourself two questions: 'Who prepared this for me to eat?' and 'Where did it come from in the first place?' Don't take it for granted – others would be very grateful for what you have!

Football

see also Balance, Fitness, Sport

What a fantastic game it is! Most young men love watching, playing, and talking about the good game (but we forgive you if you don't!). There are great games to be seen every season. Premiership teams go up and down and players change teams. Managers make mistakes and referees go temporarily blind every match! It's great to follow football, the nation's favourite sport.

But there are problems too. If football becomes an obsession, then it has got out of control, taking the place of God in your life. If football becomes the only thing you are interested in on a Sunday, then where is worship and church? Football values people wrongly, making it appear that we are only worth what others will pay for us. And remember that some of your friends, and girls too, may be really bored by football and endless soccer talk! It is great, it is exciting and it is worth following . . . but it isn't likely to be your whole life, so don't let it take over!

Forgiveness

When did you last have to forgive someone who had hurt you? When did someone last forgive you? Life is full of mistakes and forgiveness, and we have to learn to be able to put the past behind us and forgive others as we hope they will forgive us. This isn't easy if the hurt or insult has cut deep or if it's been going on for a long time. But carrying unforgiveness is like having a little bit of you going rotten inside, and it won't get better until you get rid of it!

Forgiveness is what God does for us. Every day, as we make mistakes, God forgives us and makes us clean again through Jesus, who carried all that wrong on to the cross. And, as we pray, we confess to God all the things we've messed up this time, and we know that as we do that, he promises to forgive. We don't deserve it, but that's a loving God for you!

Gg

Gangs

see also Peers, Youth Groups

Most people have groups of friends around them. Generally they share the same interests and hobbies, have fun telling jokes and hanging out in the same place, and get on really well. But gangs are a little different.

You may have been in a gang when you were younger, and it was really fun to feel that you belonged. But gangs of teenage boys are not the same things at all. Many gangs see it as fun to exclude others who don't fit for reasons of colour, ability or family background. Gangs can intimidate others, particularly more vulnerable people such as children or the elderly. Gangs can easily get drawn into acts of vandalism. Gangs don't have a valuable part to play in the life of a community and they are made up of people who are scared to be individuals.

It's right for you to meet and mix with peers, and it's healthy to have fun with a group of others. But if that group starts to become a gang, it's best to get out of it.

Gay

see also Masturbation, Sex

The word 'gay' means homosexual. Some experts say that one in every ten men is actually gay, although not all are in gay relationships. Some of your friends may be wondering if they are gay, feeling attractions to other boys that they know are not what they should be feeling.

It is normal for some boys to be attracted to other boys, particularly older ones, while they go through puberty and move towards being men. In most cases this soon passes and is replaced by a desire to get to know girls. But for a few the feelings linger and the attractions grow stronger.

God's ideal is that men and women get together, but if you feel attracted to other boys don't worry – you're not a freak and God still loves you. For your own safety it's best to avoid any physical or sexual contact with other boys, and it would be worth talking to an adult you trust such as your youth group leader.

Girls

see also Girlfriends, Women

The female of the race, blessed with shapely figures, long hair and high voices! You may or may not be dead keen on anything female, but you've got to admit that they certainly are different!

Girls have their own problems to contend with at the same time as you're going through your teenage traumas. Part of becoming a woman means that they get moody and feel ill from time to time. They also worry about relationships, spots, self-image and the other problems that life throws their way. They mature a bit sooner and quicker than us males, so they are likely to look down on their peer males and have crushes on older boys . . . sorry!

Girls are still fun to be with, even if, like you, they don't quite seem to know what to do with the body that is developing under their noses. Don't be too keen to get a special girl all for yourself, because if you are, you'll never know what the others have to offer!

Girlfriends

see also Girls, Valentines, Women

Look, there's no rush! You are not in a race to be the first lad in the youth group to have a girlfriend, and it's not always as good as you imagine anyway. But if you do feel it's time to ask a girl out, you'll need a lot of courage, a bit of privacy and the strength to cope if she says 'No way, I'd rather go out with a gorilla!'

If all goes well and you get your girl, be careful – they are delicate and so are you. Look after your girlfriend, do nothing to upset her and make sure that she's as bothered about you as you are about her. Don't rush into snogging – let time pass and get to know each other first. Don't spend every last penny on her Valentine's Day present, but do get her something nice. And remember that, while it's unlikely that she's the girl you will end up spending the rest of your life with, she is at least willing to put up with you for a while, and that can't be bad!

God

see also Bible, Faith, Jesus, Religions

The Creator of everything, the beginning and the end, the holy and righteous one . . . God is so much! That's why it's so amazing that the God who made everything and has it all to look after can care about individuals like you and me.

There's a great deal about God that humans will never understand and a lot more that we try to understand but struggle with. We might wonder why God bothered sending his Son to die for people who took no notice of him, yet he did. We might not understand why God cares in the slightest about the problems we face, yet he does.

There are answers to some questions about God, and it's worth reading books and asking people who can help you find the answers.

God cares about you more than you will ever care about anyone! The only other question is whether you really care about God, and that's one for you to answer.

Good News

see also Boasting

It's a great feeling to get good news. You might have won something, passed an important test or heard that someone special is coming to see you. You might even have heard a girl say 'Yes' when you asked her out! Good news makes us want to jump around, tell everyone and celebrate big scale!

Despite some of the downs you go through, life is great. There are plenty of times when good things happen, and generally life is pretty good without special moments. But don't be too loud about your successes – you know how it feels to be down when someone else is on the up! Just be grateful to God for the good news and make life for those at home a little easier.

Grandparents

see also Family, Relations

Grey power is all the rage! Grandparents are no longer the frail old people who can't remember your name! Grandparents have lots to offer you, if you take time to listen. They have experiences which can help you make your decisions. They have all the gossip on when your parents were young, which has got to be worth something!

Grandparents are usually amazingly ignorant of their grandchildren's failings and amazingly positive about their successes! They are there to spoil you, look after you and give you far too much. They provide some light relief when your parents get too much for you. They like to spend time with you, but don't have the responsibility of having you to look after the rest of the time.

They do a lot for you, and therefore you should let them know that you appreciate it. Tell them you love them, give them something that surprises them, or simply dress in a tidy item of clothing when you see them. Most of all, don't write off the grey power!

Growing

see also Cleanliness, Hormones, Voice, Zits

Why is it that we can't just go to bed one evening as a boy and wake up the following morning as a man? That would be much easier than all this puberty and adolescence stuff! As you grow, things start to happen to you that are, to say the least, a little unfortunate! You develop legs and arms that would look more fitting on a monkey, and your voice does all sorts of odd things while you're trying to talk intelligently to the most attractive girls around! Hair appears where hair does not belong, and awful smells erupt from under arms after a warm day. Hair becomes greasy and seems to have died a tragic death, skin becomes greasy enough to fry an egg on, and spots descend from outer space to cover the face, neck and chest.

There's nothing to be said that can change the reality of teenage manhood. These things will pass, and all your mates will go through them too. It's all part of growing up, although you may want to ask God why when you finally make it to heaven!

Hh

Hair

see also Cleanliness

Apart from the hair which grows in other places, which you are probably becoming increasingly aware of but which looks after itself, there's also the hair on your head and face to worry about.

As you go through your teenage changes, your hair is likely to be a bit more greasy and lifeless than usual and needs some special attention. You may be wise to change your shampoo and make sure you rinse your hair properly after you have washed it.

Facial hair also needs some attention. This is where a chat with your dad or an older guy really proves useful. Shaving is a skill, and there are sure to be mistakes in the early days. Shaving with a battery or electric razor can leave a rash and has to be done when the skin is clean and dry . . . which is just about never! Wet shaving with an exposed blade is asking for trouble, especially if you also have spots to contend with. Get help and advice, before it's too late.

Finally, as you look in the mirror and see your greasy hair resembling an overgrown bush and your face covered in plasters from shaving mistakes, remember that God loves you just like that . . . unbelievable but true!

Hang-Ups

see Fears

Heroes

see also Faith, Jesus

There's something good about having someone to look up to. If your bedroom is a normal teenage one, there will be posters on the wall of heroes of one kind or another. There may be sporting heroes, football players and pop stars.

Heroes help us look at ourselves and dream about what we could be when we are older. They can be a spur to get working, training or aiming at higher and better things. We are right to admire the abilities and skills which others have and to model ourselves on them. But it's also worth remembering that no hero is as perfect as we might think, and there are things about all of them which we would be silly to copy. The only true hero is a man who cared ceaselessly for others and was cheered wherever he went. He had the guts to stand up against wrong and evil, was humiliated and battered, and carried his own cross up the hillside. There he died for everyone. Now that's some hero!

Holidays

see also Family, Home Life

Holidays can be brilliant, and they can be a nightmare! Everyone goes on holiday wanting different things, and often families come to blows over what to do before a couple of days have passed. If you have to go on family holidays, you might find that there's nothing to do, or that everyone wants to do things which you think are boring. Holidays like that are a real test of your patience and tolerance of others, but it's best for everyone if you try to keep a lid on your frustrations.

There are now so many Christian holidays, camps and missions that you need never be bored again! You may want to go on your own or with a group of friends. Either way, they are designed with you in mind and include activities which you want to do. Then there's really good worship and teaching which can't be got anywhere else! God wants us to rest; it's good to rest and it's fun to rest!

Homelessness

see also Home Life

There are people who prefer not to have a stable home, but they are not normal homeless people. The majority of people who sleep on the streets, in parks or in squats have suffered problems at home, at work or school, and have not been able to find anywhere to live. Many teenagers who run away from home because it's not working well for them end up homeless, and unless they are quickly spotted and helped by people who really care, they end up at great personal risk. Homeless teenage lads are prey to those who want to get them into drugs and crime, or want them to become part of the 'sex' trade. Homelessness is lonely, sad and dangerous.

Christians have a responsibility to care for people who're having a bad time and do all we can to provide for them. Your church or a church in your area may do some work with homeless people, and it would be great if there's a way you can help while keeping safe.

Home Life

see also Bedrooms, Family, Parents

Life at home depends on everyone who lives there to work together. It isn't going to work if your mum does all the work, or your little brother gets all the attention. It's going to fail if you have teenage tantrums all the time, stamp upstairs and play your music so loud that your friends two miles away can hear it!

Home life is a lesson in tolerance, sensitivity and endurance. You take home your problems with girls and your struggles with school work, as well as the hormonal moods which are part of teenage boyhood. Your dad and mum may bring home their worries about money and tiredness after a day at work. Your sister or brother may bring home far too much energy or a really bad mood. Home is where you can be yourself, zits and all! Put it all together and there's a recipe for disaster, unless everyone takes a step back and considers the others.

Home may be an unpleasant or even painful place for you to go. Families that are under pressure sometimes struggle and fail, and you may not want to face the arguments and tensions again. If you're in a difficult home situation, talk it and pray it through, and trust God to see you through the difficulties that you face.

Homework

see also Deadlines, School, Teachers

There is no way to avoid it. When you come home from school, it's there in your bag, and, no matter how hard you try to ignore the work, it simply will not go away!

Homework is one of the boring chores of life that have to be done. It may be best for you to go straight home and get on with it, leaving the rest of the evening free for real life, real friends and unreal TV! If you don't understand your homework, make sure you ask your teacher what to do until you do understand it. If you're at home and struggling, try making a short phone call to a friend and asking them for a bit of advice. You might even consider asking your parents – you may be surprised by their knowledge, and, if nothing else, it makes the poor old people feel wanted! And don't store up homework until 9 o'clock on Sunday night unless you want to get really bad marks!

Hormones

see also Growing

These wild things go a little mad in teenagers and make life difficult for those around you. Hormones make you suddenly show interest in anything in a skirt (but hopefully not a kilted Scotsman!), and they're responsible for many of those physical changes. Hormones also help make you moody and irritable, and they turn you into the youth from hell every now and again. Your parents will look at you with fear in their eyes as if you've just escaped from the zoo, and you will find yourself going completely and utterly OTT over nothing at all. The odd thing is that you'll probably not realise just what a monster you're becoming until the phase has passed!

To cope with some of these hormonal nightmares you must try to have space to yourself, don't let silly little things get to you, and walk away if you feel yourself brewing up for an explosion. You will survive reasonably unscathed eventually, honest!

Ii

Illness

see also Operations

Illness and sickness are part of life and we'll all suffer from time to time. Most illnesses come and go and we get over them quickly, but that's not always the case. There are people who suffer long bouts of illness, have to go to hospital for frequent stays, and never seem to be properly well and enjoying good health.

Your mum will remember times when you were younger when she sat up all night with you while you suffered an illness, and she is naturally and rightly concerned when you are ill now that you are older.

It's not easy to cope with being ill, and it's easy to feel very sorry for yourself. God promises to be with us in all times of need, and as well as healing through prayer, he heals through medicines, drugs and other people too. When you get ill, see it as a chance to have a rest and be looked after, instead of a time to feel frustrated and down.

Independence

see also Abilities, Self-Worth, Work

'I don't need you – I can manage on my own.' So goes the cry of son to father in homes across the country. Growing up is about learning to cope on your own, doing things without help and support, and trying to prove things to yourself. Independence is something you may yearn for, wanting to be free from home, rules and restrictions. But, like many things, it carries problems and burdens too.

Being independent may mean never having others to turn to and having to rely on yourself for everything. It could mean not wanting to ask for assistance because you lose face, or people will say 'I told you so'. It's good to want to do as much as you can for yourself, but it's a sign that you've really grown up when you admit you can't do everything on your own and you ask for help.

Individuality

see also Fashion, Peers, Responsibility

Do you want to be seen as part of a crowd or as an individual? Peers and fashions can force you to do what everyone else does, dress in the same way, go to the same places and do the same things. But that doesn't allow room for you to be you!

God's so clever that he never made anyone else quite like you. You've got your own body, your own face and facial expressions, your own personality and your own character. Your individuality is something to thank God for and celebrate, not hide or cover up. You don't need to give up all that's special about you in order to be accepted by others.

Your individual faith can be hard to be open about. There are those who find it funny to tease Christians, and others who will ridicule you for speaking openly about what you believe. But standing up for God shows clearly that you are an individual capable of making your own decisions – and you have a better trend to follow!

Internet

see also Computer Games, Email, Social Networking

The internet is a great source of knowledge and information. It has revolutionised homework and research. There's a wealth of stuff out there just waiting for you to find it.

Not everything the internet has to offer is healthy. There are adverts for things which you can't afford, and chat-sites which lead you to spend too much time logged on. And there are things of evil and other unhelpful words and images floating around ready to be found. Like all good things, the internet should be used with care, and if you're not sure about something, get out of it and ask advice. Then it will remain the great resource that it should be and not a dangerous one.

Jj

Jealousy

see also Forgiveness

Many friendships are damaged by jealousy as it eats away like an insect, poisoning attitudes and making unimportant things seem vital.

There are few of us who could honestly say that we've not been jealous of someone or something. You may be jealous of other boys who are clever, better at football or more attractive to the girls than you are. You may get jealous of your brothers or sisters, thinking that they are getting more love and attention than you are. It's strange to think that the person you're jealous of is quite possibly jealous of you! Whatever your weakness, jealousy is a huge waste of time and energy, and the only one who really suffers is you! Give it to God, ask for peace and then get on with your life.

Jesus

see also Bible, Faith, God, Religions

Son of God and Saviour. Although he is part of God, he lived and suffered as you do, faced problems as you do, and died a horrible death as you probably won't! Jesus was not the wet, wimpish figure we so often see in pictures – he was strong, hard and very brave. He suffered physical abuse and torture amazingly, and died with dignity on the cross with blood pouring from him. He was more than a great man and has more than a little interest in your life and your future. The same Jesus who walked in Palestine and looked up to see Zacchaeus in the tree is with you now and sees you in just the same way.

Jesus is the central figure of Christianity and has changed the world through changing people's lives. He is willing to change your life if you haven't been changed by him already. If you're even a bit as strong as he is, you'll ask him.

Jobs at Home

see also Family, Home Life, Kitchen, Laziness

Someone has to do all the things that go to make a home run properly. There are jobs which parents will naturally do, and others which they would never expect you to have a go at. But there are probably also jobs which you are asked to do and you do everything to avoid having to!

If you don't have to do any jobs at home you are being a little bit spoiled and you are not being helped to grow independent and look after yourself. Why should others do everything that makes you comfortable, well-dressed and well-fed? The justice that God expects us to live by means that we've all got a part to play and no one has a right to expect it all to be done for them.

It's more likely that you have jobs to do, and that you argue with your siblings about whose turn it is. At times it won't be fair and you will end up doing more than your share, but could you honestly say that you do more jobs around the home than your mum? Whenever jobs need doing, it's much safer to get on with them quietly and without too much fuss; otherwise more jobs might appear as well!

Kk

Kissing

see also Girlfriends, Love, Sex

Having a quick snog behind the bike sheds is not what a loving relationship should be about! Kissing is something that is a natural part of a relationship that's starting to mean something to both you and the victim (or should that be your young lady?!). There is no great and magical formula to make kissing better, and there's not a lot of point discussing it widely with your friends either before or after the event. Kissing is only special when it's meant to be special – when two people are showing their affection for each other in a loving way. And remember – girls don't particularly like passionate kisses for a long time and until they are really sure about you, so keep your tongue to yourself!

Kitchen

see also Food, Home Life

Have you heard of it? It's the room where food is prepared in most homes. It's the room where at least one of your parents spends a great deal of time washing, tidying, cooking and clearing up for you. You may not think much of the room itself, and you may not often show that you think much of the person who virtually lives in there either!

A lot of work goes on in your home which you don't do and are not asked to do. When was the last time you thanked those who look after your needs and showed them that you don't really take it all for granted? And when was the last time you thanked God for your comforts?

Ll

Late Nights *see also Arguments, Parents, Rules*

There's a whole new language associated with teenagers and late nights! There are phrases like 'And not a minute after' and 'Where have you been to until this hour?' which are only ever said by anxious parents scared about the late night that their son is enjoying. The problem is that you don't understand how worried parents get about you staying out late. And they don't understand what it's like to have to go home just as you and your mates are having a good time.

Late nights cause so much grief in families, and the only way to avoid the hassle is to be patient, listen to the other point of view, and discuss it like the adult you keep telling them you are! Parents do care – they're not just trying to spoil your fun. They know that eventually you will be too tired to live your life properly if you spend too much night-time out and not enough getting your beauty sleep! Remember that even your parents were young once, even if it was centuries ago!

Laziness

see also Jobs at Home, Work

There's a difference between resting and being lazy. There are always things to be done in your bedroom or around the house, and there's homework in your school bag. The problem is that whenever your brain tells you to get on with the work your body decides it must slump on to the settee and watch TV.

Laziness doesn't help anyone. If you're lazy at home, you're going to get stick, and rightly so. Why should your parents work their nylon socks off to keep you in the lazy lifestyle to which you're becoming accustomed? If you've got a job and you're lazy, you'll soon find that others will take the work and wages from you. If you're lazy at school, it will be noted, and you're not doing yourself any favours anyway. Laziness is not a physical problem – it's a messy state of mind. Beat it before it beats you!

Leadership

see also Abilities

As you get older, you'll see adults in positions of responsibility, such as church leaders or teachers, and you'll respect some of them for the way they take the lead and you'll not rate others at all! This is great, because it shows that you're beginning to understand what it means to be a leader.

Young men are needed to be leaders at school, church, youth group and all sorts of other places. Younger boys need others to look up to, whom they can respect and want to be like. You're probably not aware of it but boys may already look up to you and want to follow your example.

If God has given you leadership skills, you need to take every opportunity to develop those and learn from your mistakes. You never know what and who God may want you to lead in the future!

Leaving

see also Fear, Independence

Moving on is always a time of mixed emotions. There are the positive challenges, experiences and discoveries to be made. There's also the pain of saying goodbye to the people and situations that you'll be leaving behind.

Leaving an area and moving house is considered one of the most stressful experiences that life has to offer. But there's no need to think that you can't build up new friendships, find a good church and search out a new youth group in your new area. It's got a number of advantages too. Your new friends won't know some of the daft and embarrassing things you've done in the past and will see you as more perfect than they see themselves. You will have the opportunity to prove yourself to a new bunch of people. And let's not forget the fresh field of girls who will be interested in the new bloke at the group! You'll be OK, with good memories of the past and good experiences of the present.

Lottery

You shouldn't buy lottery tickets until you're 18, although you may do so already. If you were to buy one ticket twice a week, you would be precisely £104 worse off than people who don't buy tickets at all! It's a mug's game for all but the very few who win something, and your chances of winning are about fourteen million to one!

The lottery has other warnings to us as Christians. It relies on chance, whereas God calls us to rely on him. It encourages people to waste money, when that money could be better spent helping others. And it's based on the worldly obsession with money and greed. Most people in developed countries have more than enough, yet we eagerly grab every chance to get a little more. If you really must throw money away like that, throw it at a homeless person instead!

Love

see also Girlfriends, Sex

Love is strong and powerful. Love is what you've experienced at home all the years since you were born, and it's the special bond you have with a friend you really trust. Love is the will to give anything for others and to go a little further than is normal to help. Love is what God lavishes on us, unending and overflowing. Love is Jesus dying on the cross and saying, 'I did it for you. Now all you have to do is love me.'

Love is the real thing. Love is what happens when you think you've met the girl of your dreams. It stops the heart, makes the stomach get butterflies and clogs up the brain with thoughts of only one person. It makes you walk home late at night in the rain and not notice that you haven't got your coat on! Love causes you to like mushy things like flowers and hearts. Love is the security of knowing that you can trust someone else fully and completely and that neither of you is holding anything back. Real love is something you will only know when you experience it.

But love is cheapened by the way we use the word. So to put the record straight, here are a few other things about love. Love is not something you make, love is not lust, love is not sex, and love is not cheap.

Mm

Magazines

There are many magazines on the market aimed at the teenage market. You may well buy some of them yourself. You may also get other magazines about cars, computers or other interests. But you will probably have noticed that boys' mags are not nearly as interesting as some of the girls' ones!

Teenage magazines have good things to offer and very dodgy things too. They are often dominated by articles, photo features and problem pages about relationships and sex. They don't always give the sort of advice that is helpful or right. They encourage young people like you to get into relationships with girls before you may want to or before you've found a girl you really like. Mags usually contain horoscopes which seem like fun but are criticised in the Bible. They are full of adverts and can make you think that you're only of value if you wear the latest clothes or have the coolest shades. So don't throw them all out just in case they damage you, but do read them with caution, asking yourself, 'What does God think about this?'

Marriage

see also Divorce, Love

They sometimes go well, they sometimes go wrong. Your grandparents may have been married for many years; your parents may have only lasted a few. Because over one in three marriages end unhappily there are more and more people suggesting that marriage is outdated and living together is a better option.

God rates marriage. He invented it so that both man and woman can feel secure and be able to trust each other. The vows made during the wedding service are commitments for life, not just until it gets too hard to bother to try or until someone else comes along. Marriage is God's ideal situation for children to grow up secure and happy. Marriage takes work, a sense of humour, heaps of forgiveness and lots of patience.

Marriage should be for life, so it's something that should be gone into only when you're really sure. You need time to enjoy yourself as an individual first before tying yourself to someone else. And marriage is no answer to problems, so don't think of it as the easy option. But good marriages can be great, exciting, comforting and really good to see as well as experience.

Masturbation

see also Gay, Love, Sex

Now to the nitty-gritty! You will already know what this is about in physical terms. As your body changes, your penis can become erect for no apparent reason, but this usually passes. However, there may have been times when, in private, you have masturbated until you reach a climax and sperm comes from the tip. Young men get a great deal of satisfaction from masturbation, and it releases some of the hormone-induced desire to be sexually active before your body and emotions are really ready. Despite what you may have heard, it does not cause blindness, your penis does not wear out, and it does no damage to your wrists!

Masturbation has its problems, and there are many Christians who say that it is completely wrong. As your sperm is capable of fertilising an egg in a female's womb, there are those who see wasting sperm as a form of killing a potential child.

Other Christians have concerns about the act itself. It is a private and personal thing to do, yet relationships are not personal and private in that way and it would be better to spend time building up friendships. Masturbation can become habit-forming and therefore almost an addiction. When you do it you may think of girls or women and fantasise about them, or look at magazines with 'sexy' pictures in. Yet God didn't make anyone to be objects thought of and used in that way.

You are not doing anything that other boys aren't doing, and so you shouldn't worry that you are in some way weird. But do think about the downsides too, and talk to an adult you trust to find out their point of view. And don't forget that you can be honest with Jesus about anything, including this.

Men

see also Growing, Independence, Women

You are aiming to be a man and your body is doing all it can to take you there. You are probably looking forward to the strength and power that men appear to have and the things that make up being a man.

Manhood is changing. Men are not always the main wage-earners in many households, and some stay at home to look after the house and children while the woman goes to work. Men can no longer be guaranteed work in traditional industries, and many older men find it hard to accept that things are changing. You are growing up in a new world with new attitudes about what men and women should be like. Men are now more able to share the work of looking after babies, to show their feelings, and to be sensitive and kind instead of hard and macho. God values men and women equally and can use us just the same. So don't allow yourself to try to become what you think people expect of a man – just be the person God made you, and he'll do the rest.

Misery

see also Depression

There are days when everything seems miserable, from the cat to the weather. You might know the misery of being chucked by a girl or failing a test at school. You will certainly know the misery of having nowhere to go and no money to spend on a wet Saturday.

Misery is a common feeling amongst everyone. With those eccentric hormones of yours, however, you may have to face up to misery more often that others do. Misery is not serious and it soon passes, except in the case of a few teachers you may know! Misery is not the same as depression, which goes deeper, lasts longer and usually needs treatment. If you want to see how the Bible treats misery, read a few Psalms. They are often about people who feel at the end of everything, yet they all come to realise that God does love them and will help them in the end.

If you are feeling miserable, it may be best for you to find a little space and try to avoid passing it on to others around you, because the more miserable they are, the more miserable you will become! And do try to smile . . . just a little!

Mobile Phones

see also Phones

Everyone seems to have a mobile these days! They are a great way to keep in touch with others in the fast life that so many people lead. You will be nagging your parents for one sooner or later.

Mobiles are useful but not usually vital. Many schools ban them because too many pupils get calls during lessons. Parents are faced with the cost of replacement when a mobile is lost. They are expensive to run and almost impossible to get repaired. It's even suspected that the radiation they give off slowly fries the brain! Too often they are a status symbol and everyone has to have one, which is one very good reason why you shouldn't go along with the crowd and follow the trend! Most of all, they intrude into moments of quiet and cut right across private and personal conversations.

Money

see also Poverty, Wants

When you're a teenager, money always seems to be in short supply and the lack of it seriously damages your social life! But however much you have, it'll never be quite enough. Parents will genuinely give you all they can, but you cost a lot! Ever since they were putting you in Pampers you have added to the family expenses. You are fed, watered, washed and clothed. You have somewhere to live and lots of possessions. You may be given pocket money and you're certainly bought presents from time to time. You are taken on holiday, and your school and youth group trips are paid for. After all that, is it really fair for you to try to tap them for some more?

Money really doesn't grow on trees (thanks, Dad!), and you may have to find your own honest way of getting some more. You could take on some part-time or Saturday work, or sell some of the things you don't want or have grown out of. You may even want to sell your little sister, but she probably wouldn't raise much! If you're getting all you can get, then you can either spend every day feeling frustrated, impoverished and miserable or make the most of what you have and spend it wisely. The best option is obvious, isn't it!

Mothers

see also Home Life, Kitchen, Parents

Think about how much your mother has gone through for you. Start before you were born and the pain of giving birth. Then think of the time she invested in you when you were small. Now she looks after you, she's always there, she tries to keep the family together, she tries to be fair, and she still loves you.

There are times when mothers seem to get too worked up about things and ask too many questions about what you're doing and where you're going. That's not because your mother is nosy or trying to spoil your fun. Fact is that mothers have a special concern for their sons and your mum is really concerned about you. Don't take for granted the love your mother offers through the way she looks after you, and be grateful that she cares!

Music

It's fact that your parents are not going to like the sort of music you like, and it's also fact that you are going to despise their sad musical tastes! Music grows up and develops for the generation it belongs to, and although your parents grew up in the 60s and 70s when pop music was going through a massive range of wild and wacky phases, they will never really get into what you like. Converting parents to your music isn't likely to happen, so instead play it out of their way and don't induce arguments by playing it too loud!

Some music is associated with particular fashions or appearance. Goths like certain types of music, punks are still around with their particular fashions, and there's a bit of concern around about the depressing music and poetry of emos. Be careful that you don't lose who you are in all the cultural stuff around certain groups or styles.

The music you listen to can have an effect on how you think and feel. If you listen to loud aggressive music, you can become loud and aggressive. If the lyrics you listen to are immoral or insults to God, then you should think again about the content of what goes in your ears. But don't be too worried about it all – music is a gift from God, a great way to relax and really fun to create.

Nn

Names

see also Individuality, Parents

Do you hate your name? Have you tried to persuade your friends to call you something else? It's no fun to be landed with a name that you hate or initials which spell out a joke for everyone. But if you ask your parents, you'll probably find that they thought long and hard about what to call you and did their best to give you a name that they hoped you'd grow to like. Many of us have shortened our names or are known by nicknames anyway.

It's worth finding out what your name means from a baby names book. In the Bible most names had a meaning, so if yours is a name from God's book, and many boy names are, then you might find there's more behind your name than you thought.

Nervousness

see also Fears, Individuality

Key times you may get nervous include before exams, when you're about to perform and when you're planning to ask a girl out. Other times may include when you've been found out and you know your dad is waiting to have a little chat!

Nervousness causes a rush of adrenaline to pulse through your veins. It also ties your stomach in knots, makes you feel wobbly and makes your head float around! To cope with a bad case, take lots of long breaths of air, try to eat even if you don't feel like it, and pray.

Oo

Occult

see also Evil, X Files

There are people who think evil, witches and the occult are fascinating and try to find out more. Some of your friends may have tried to involve you in occult practices like ouija boards and fortune telling.

Evil is real in the world and there are things which we will never understand. But there's plenty of evidence that people who start to dabble in occult things can end up having problems. Some live in fear and are scared to go out, and others are unable to sleep because they are too scared of the dreams they have. This is one thing where the only thing to do is to walk away. If you've been involved in the past, or you have friends who've messed around, then pray and talk to adults about it. You need God to clear out the evil that might have crept in.

Operations

see also Illness

Most of us will never have to suffer under the surgeon's knife, but we may know of people who do. Perhaps parents, other relatives or friends have had to go into hospital and have themselves chopped open.

Operations are another way that God heals us. He made us and he knows how we work, yet even so sometimes we go wrong. Skilled surgeons are trained to sort these problems out without fainting at all that blood and gore! God is in control, so if you are facing an operation, remember to pray, and if you know someone else who is, ask whether you can pray for them too.

Pp

Parents

see also Fathers, Home Life, Mothers

Mothers, fathers, step-parents, foster-parents . . . parents come in all shapes and sizes. Sometimes they are the kindest, most loving people who ever lived, and at other times they resemble the evil dead!

Parents are not out to ruin your life, even if what they say and do seems to point that way. They care about what you do with your time and money, they want you to work hard and do well for yourself, and they want you to be fit and well by washing and sleeping enough. They also make mistakes, get the wrong end of the stick and over-react when you do relatively minor things. When they're having a go, try to listen and to think rather than argue, and then quietly put your point of view. Most of all, remember that not everyone has parents who care as much as yours, so be thankful!

Parties

see also Booze, Drugs, Peers, Sex

There's plenty in life to celebrate. Parties are one way to enjoy life and let your hair down. Parties can be great fun, and they can be disasters.

How you feel about going to a party depends on what mood you're in, whether you know the people there, and whether you're likely to see people you don't want to see such as an ex-girlfriend. It can be hard to walk into a room full of strangers and try to enjoy yourself.

Parties at home while your parents are away are never a good idea. Think about the possible damage to furniture, who is going to take control if you are overrun with gatecrashers, and what the neighbours will tell your parents! Don't even think about it!

Parties have other risks which any teenage lad will think about, and if you know you will be tempted to get involved in things you shouldn't, then it may be best not to go. There may be drink flowing and drugs available. Others may be getting into meaningless and sad sexual activity. What sort of Christian example are you giving by going to parties you know are not good? If you go too far into these things, be sure that your friends will never stop reminding you how stupid you were, and you will also feel guilty for a long time. Don't lose control.

Peers

see also Friends, Individuality

We all need a group of friends around us to grow up with, to help us out and to talk things through. Youth groups are really good at providing a place where you can meet others going through the same things as you are.

Peers at school and elsewhere may put pressure on you to do certain things or behave in a particular way. They may suggest that unless you are wearing this or that brand of trainers or sportswear you are not cool enough. They may push you to get into smoking, drink or drugs because they all say they do it and they seem fine. They may boast about their often-imagined sexual experience and make you feel you're being left behind.

It's hard to swim against the tide of your peers, but if you're wise and you're strong, that's exactly what you'll do. You're an individual and you've got a good brain with which to make your own decisions. You've got a God who wants to give you the strength to be different and stand up for what you know is true and right. There's no point in being swept along with all the others and becoming like a clone of them.

Perfection

see also Abilities, Individuality, Self-Worth

You are not perfect, the Queen is not perfect, no one is perfect. Even the girl you fancy isn't perfect, although she's probably pretty close!

We are fed images of perfection in magazines, on TV and throughout life. Perfect men have six-pack stomachs, cheesy white-teeth grins, cool clothes and adoring women surrounding them. Perfect teenage lads are healthy, spot-free, sun-tanned and fantastically attractive. They are not zit-covered, greasy-haired, uncoordinated, scruffily dressed and permanently embarrassed.

The sort of perfection the world feeds us is not real, so don't get hung up about it. It's good to aim to be fit, to take care of yourself and to take pride in what you wear, but you will never be exactly perfect in your own eyes or in the eyes of the world. But you are perfect to God, and you will appear pretty near perfect to the girl who eventually decides you are the one for her.

Pets

Many families have pets around, and they can be cute and loving. They can also be dirty, embarrassing and very badly behaved! You may have a dog that loves attacking people as they come in, or a cat that leaves little 'messages' on the carpet which you find in the morning as you walk around bare-foot! Or perhaps you have had a succession of hamsters and gerbils that have all died for no apparent reason after a few weeks.

If you have a pet, don't forget that it's your responsibility to care for it. They can become friends and are at least something you can talk to that won't answer back or offer naff advice! But pets need to be clean, they need veterinary attention and check-ups, they need to be fed and watered frequently, and they need exercise. As part of God's creation they deserve respect and care in the same way that we are cared for.

Phones

see also Mobile Phones

The ultimate question about the phone is 'Who pays the bill?' Yes, you want to talk to your friends all the time and you must spend a couple of hours each evening logging on and seeing who has emailed you, but it all costs your parents money.

The phone is a great way to keep in touch and a cool way of wasting time and money. It's fun to talk on the phone after school but your homework is still waiting to be done when you put the phone down. You would also be amazed at how long a quick chat to a mate can take on the phone – time yourself sometime.

If you want to be able to use the phone more or less when you want to, then you need to think about suggesting two things to your parents. You could offer to pay for your calls, or you could suggest that another line is installed for you to pay for and use. These options will cost you money, but there's no way your parents can be expected to cough up for your endless chats for ever. And whatever you do, remember that while you're on the phone you're not doing more important things.

Popularity

see also Boasting, Self-Worth

Some people are naturally popular and others are not. It's not usually about their appearance or intelligence, it's just something they have that attracts others to them.

Popular teenage lads are at a real advantage. They are likely to get away with more at school than others. They are likely to have the pick of the girls and be able to be choosy rather than desperate. They don't have to try too hard at anything. Yet popular people are also in a fishbowl – others are always watching them to see what they do and how they do it.

If you are popular, thank God for it and pray that it'll last. If you don't think you're popular, don't worry – God loves you, so does your family and so do your friends.

Poverty

see also Money, Wants

No, this is not the state you are in! Although you might not have the money to buy a new pair of trainers today, at least you have a home and food coming your way in a few hours. You may feel you are impoverished sometimes, but it's like the difference between hungry for a biscuit and starving for the first meal in weeks – poles apart!

Poverty exists as a reality in pockets of our country and in all of the developing countries in the world. Suffering in the form of avoidable illnesses brought on by poor water or sanitation is combined with a complete lack of money for people to use to help themselves. People struggle to get by on very little or nothing, and become reliant on what other nations and states can offer them. Poverty means having literally nothing. God didn't want the world to be this way, and we should all be looking for ways we can help address the problem.

Prayer

see also God, Worship

Prayer is a fantastic gift from God which we should make the most of by doing it regularly. Through prayer we can communicate with him directly, and only through communication can relationships really develop and become strong.

We can pray to God at any time and in any place. We can ask for things, thank him for things and say sorry for things. God doesn't mind if we use prayers that we read out, say prayers that we've learned, or speak to him in our own words like we would to a friend.

Prayer is about honesty. If you are honest to God about how you feel and what you are going through, he will listen. Remember that Jesus came to suffer and live as we do so that he knows the struggles that life throws up. You can tell God everything that you couldn't even tell your best friend or your parents. Prayer is the ultimate in communication. Do it!

Pressure

You may have loads of pressure being placed on you at the mo. There could be pressure to do well or work harder at school, pressure from parents to choose a career that they want you to do, and pressure to live in a way that you know God wouldn't like. Teenage lads' life is about learning to cope with pressure, making decisions for yourself, and working out what is best for you rather than what is best for other people.

Peer pressure – that's your friends trying to make you do the stupid things they do – is tough to stand against. But if you know they want you to do wrong, whether against the law, against God's plan or against your conscience, then you know what you've got to do!

Life as a man will have all those pressures, and now is a good time to start to learn to deal with pressure.

Puberty

see Adolescence, Hormones

Qq

Questions

see also Doubts

Life is full of questions, and sadly we will never know the answer to some. When you were about 5 you probably went through a phase of asking questions all the time, and after each answer asking 'Why?' again. Now your questions are a little more sophisticated and you expect more from the answers.

You're right to ask questions – it shows that you've got a brain and you're willing to use it. But don't expect answers to everything. Ask questions of your parents, your youth leader, church leader or older relatives. Find out what they think about issues that are bugging you. But don't forget God too. If you believe that he made everything, then he's the best one to answer some of the deeper questions in life. It has been said that life is all about learning, so you will always have questions to ask and answers to find.

Rr

Rejection

see also Abilities, Individuality, Popularity, Self-Worth

There are few feelings worse than being rejected. Rejection is painful, cuts very deep and lasts for quite a while.

You'll probably have to face up to rejection sooner or later. You may try to get established in a new place and find that you're not wanted. You may do something that really hurts your parents and they struggle to show their love for you for a while. Or you may go through the turmoil of asking a girl out only to be rejected by her.

Rejection goes right to the depths of how you see yourself. If you don't rate yourself anyway and you're always looking in the mirror and wishing you were different, rejection will come as no surprise but will only serve to confirm that you are useless. If you're used to success, rejection will feel like the whole world has fallen in.

You are of value, you are different from anyone else, and God made you like you are because that's how he wanted you to be. That might seem difficult to believe, but if you don't accept it, you're saying that God got it wrong!

If someone rejects you, it's their loss, not yours. Rejection doesn't happen often and can be survived. Ask

God to help you pick yourself up, dust yourself off, apologise where necessary and thrust yourself into the world again!

Relations

see also Grandparents

Just like brothers and sisters, you didn't pick them and you can't do much about them either! Relations can be great fun and dreadfully embarrassing.

Relations are the sort of people who come out with stupid comments like 'Haven't you grown!' Well, they would have been even more surprised if you had shrunk! They always want to give you a sloppy lipstick kiss, and they talk about what a handsome young man you've become and how you'll break a few hearts.

Relations mean well. They can be generous and kind, give good presents and they care about you. When you get older you won't have to see them as much unless you choose to do so, and you might be surprised just how nice they really are. They're your relations whether you like it or not, so you'd be better off making the most of it.

Religions

see also God, Faith

Real Christianity shouldn't be thought of as a religion but as a faith. Religions are about going through the motions and worshipping because that's what you have to do. Christianity is a faith based on relationship with God and Jesus and relying on power from the Holy Spirit. You have choices to make about how you live your life and how you worship.

In school and on TV you will learn a great deal about other religions. This is a good thing, because you don't have to believe it to understand what it means to follow a different religion. You may find some of the things attractive and some of them quite unbelievable. Either way, it also gives you an opportunity to speak about your faith and what it means to you to be a Christian.

As you learn about other religions, don't forget what Christianity teaches. It says that the only way to be really happy and have everlasting life is from God through Jesus. It's not popular to say that there is only one way to find God, but that's what the Bible teaches and that's what God asks us to believe.

Responsibility

see also Independence, Work

Being a teenager is like sitting on a fence. Half of you wants to enjoy being a child and having no responsibilities while the other half wants to be an adult and wants to be given more responsibilities.

You already have responsibilities. There may be times you have to look after the house or your younger siblings. You may be responsible for some jobs around the house or for keeping your room tidy. School makes you responsible for getting there, for wearing your uniform and for doing your work to the best of your ability. And there are plenty of responsibilities to come as you make decisions about your future and take on more at church or at school.

Responsibility is not always easy to carry and demands that you get advice and help when you need it. Think of the added responsibilities your parents have – they are responsible for the family and home, for staff or other things at work, roles in church and other family members. Don't be in too much of a hurry to take that lot on!

Rules

see also Home Life, Parents, School

If we didn't have any rules, everything would fall apart as people only did what suited them without any thought for others. A world without rules would be anarchy and no one would feel safe or secure.

God gave humankind rules to live by, and if everyone stuck to them, there'd be a lot less crime and pain in the world and everyone would feel safer and better.

Rules are not there to restrict but to give freedom! Rules are usually about safety, fairness and consideration. They are made for the good of everyone. If you obey rules, you'll find that life ticks on quite nicely, surprisingly free of hassle for you or anyone else. If you try to fight rules, sooner or later things will go horribly wrong for you and you'll suffer the consequences.

There might be rules at home which have been there since as long as you can remember and you think need changing. If that's the case, don't argue or throw a wobbly, but take time to talk to your parents about them. Your mature attitude may persuade them that you've got a point!

Ss

Sad

Everyone seems sad in what they do, what they wear and what they listen to – except a teenage boy! Think of your parents – they really like very sad things, they are stuck in a dreary time-warp, and they hate the things that you and your mates know are by far the coolest things on the planet!

This is normal and right. Life would be boring if we all liked the same things and if we didn't change with age. If you think back, you probably enjoyed doing things as a boy which now you think were deeply sad and you would never admit to your friends.

There's nothing wrong with being confident that what you like is best and everything else is sad. But remember, one day you'll be older and teenagers will call you sad too!

Safety

see also Aggression, Crime

There's a lot of concern around at the moment about the safety of young people. Occasionally there are unprovoked attacks on youths by other teens, and these hit the headlines. Most of the time in most places it is perfectly safe to go around, but you've got to be a bit sensible and a bit careful.

Some of the ways to keep safe are to go places with others rather than on your own, stick to the same well-lit routes at night where other people are around, and keep in touch with those at home about where you are and what you're doing. Don't carry too much money or other high-value electronic stuff with you, and be ready to run or ask adults for help if you feel in danger.

Prayer helps too! We all feel a bit scared when we're on our own and sense something's not right, but the assurance that God is with us is worth lots!

School

see also Exclusion, Homework, Teachers

The necessary evil in every teenager's life. School has plenty of downsides and negatives. School is full of rules and regulations and things are expected of you. School is a place you have to go to for 39 weeks a year for up to 14 years. School terms last for ever and school holidays are always far too short. School work can be boring, dull and difficult. School can be a place where you are bullied, humiliated or made to look foolish.

School is also the place where you are given opportunities that older people would die for! Schools have equipment, books and information on a massive range of subjects, and school is where you can lay the foundations for the rest of your life. School is where help is available, where you can try out taking on responsibility, and where there are usually masses of girls to think about and look at! School is the place you have to go to because generations have found that education matters and they are willing to spend thousands of pounds on your education every year!

School can be a pain. If you are struggling with any problems at school, talk to your parents and teachers. School is a fantastic opportunity – you'd be a fool not to give it your best shot.

Self-Worth

see also Individuality, Popularity

Many people struggle with their own self-image. They look in the mirror and wish they looked differently, could do things better or made more of a mark on the world. Teenage lads suffer a great deal as they try to find what value they are to the world, to their families or to their friends.

As you look in the mirror or lie on your bed thinking about yourself, it's important to remember that you are going through a time of great change, and the 'you' that you see now will have changed massively in four or five years' time. You will look different and sound different. You will have developed new skills and found success in new areas of life. You may have a particular girlfriend or a group of mates you enjoy spending time with. You will probably get on with your parents far better than you do now.

Whatever you're like at the moment, you are still worth a lot to God, to your family and to the others around you who value your friendship.

Sex

see also Gay, Girlfriends, Love, Masturbation, Virgin

You don't have to look far to be aware of sex. Sex is used to sell ice-cream and newspapers. Sex is on TV and videos, and images of sex are available in magazines and books. Sex is discussed openly, and we're all left with the impression that everyone is doing it except us!

Sex has got completely out of hand. Some people's need for sex means that they use others rather than really love them. The ideal of sex between man and woman has got confused and rejected. Marriages have split up because one or other of the partners wanted more sex than the marriage offered. God didn't want it to be this way.

The act of sex or 'making love' should be a very special experience between two people of opposite genders who are formally committed to each other for life through marriage. This is the only way in which they can give to one another completely without feeling used or abused by the other. Many young people have had their understanding of what sex and love really mean ruined by rushing into it before they were ready, and before the legal age of consent of 16, and they have ended up feeling cheap and used. Young people who sleep around are putting themselves in danger of catching a number of very nasty sexually-transmitted diseases and suffering the pain of heartbreak and rejection time and time again.

As a boy you have the responsibility not to force a girl to do something that she doesn't want to do and that you know you shouldn't do. You have to keep control of yourself and make sure that you're not going too far. You need to know what excites you and know when to stop yourself from getting too sexually aroused. Accidents can easily happen when cuddling goes further and the boy and girl lack self-control and sexual intercourse takes place. Ask yourself: do you feel ready to take on the responsibilities of being a father? If you think you could get over-excited, avoid being on your own in private with your girlfriend. It's not easy to understand right now, but it is worth it to wait before you get into sexual activity.

Shops

see also Fashion, Wants

Shops are either fascinating places that deserve lots of time and attention or places to avoid like the plague! If you go shopping with either your mum or your girlfriend, you may be bored to death and put off shopping for life. And there's the risk that your mates will spot you out shopping with them – deeply uncool!

Shopping is necessary occasionally and sometimes you may need to go and help. Your mum might want to find a new outfit for you, which can't really be done if you don't go with her. If you have to go shopping, you'll only make the whole experience worse if you mope around looking suicidal!

Shops show us what's available and what we haven't got. Most people see things they want but know they can't afford. Teenage lads top the polls of arrested shoplifters, usually because they saw something they didn't have the money to buy so they tried to help themselves. There are even gangs of teenagers who dare each other to go into shops and nick stuff. This is not what a teenage lad with a brain wants to get into; you'll have a police record which can affect the rest of your life.

Sisters

see also Brothers, Home Life

It all depends how old they are and how much money they've got. Sisters can be of great value to a growing young man or they can ruin his life!

Big sisters are probably better than little ones. A big sister gives you a bit of cred amongst your friends, particularly if she's attractive and free. Big sisters are likely to have mothered you and looked after you more than you really needed when you were younger. Big sisters who are earning feel themselves drawn to spoil their little brothers. OK, so they can also be cruel, embarrassing and spiteful, but so can you!

Little sisters are from another planet! They interfere with your things, play in your room without asking, and whine about you to your parents. They make fun of your changing voice and shaving cuts, and they get in the way when you bring your girlfriend round. But if they weren't around, your parents would have more time to nag you about your room or interrogate you about how you spend your money!

Good or bad, lovely or loathsome, sisters are here to stay, so try to put up with them as best you can.

Soaps

see also TV

There are plenty of soaps on TV and it's easy to get really interested in them. There are great storylines, amusing characters and teenage lads getting away with loads of things you'd like to be able to do! But soaps give a false impression of real life and set us targets which it's not possible to meet. Everything that happens in a soap in a couple of weeks would take months or years in reality. Relationships come and go all the time, and people get over knock-backs in a matter of minutes. It's not like that in the big wide world out there, so don't get the false impression that it is!

Social Networking

see also Email, Internet

The internet has quite a few social networking sites such as Bebo and MySpace where individuals can put up info on themselves, share how they feel and assemble a group of 'friends' around them.

You'll know about these and may have your own profiles. But there are dangers. Think carefully about what you publish about yourself, as it could put you in danger from people who want to falsely befriend you and abuse you. You may also say things that are upsetting or offensive to friends.

The Bible was written very, very long before these sites were invented, so it's hard to work out what God has to say about them. But we do know from what Jesus said that people and personal relationships are important, and they're not quite as real or powerful when you type words in and communicate through a screen. If you're into these, that's OK, but don't forget your real, flesh and blood family and friends!

Solvents

see also Addiction, Drugs

Abuse of solvents is becoming a serious problem with your age-group and any lad with an ounce of brain will steer well clear.

Solvent abuse is basically the sniffing of chemicals which can be found in some glues and cleaning materials. The chemicals affect the brain and induce a light-headed feeling, hallucinations and weird dreams. It is now thought that permanent damage is caused by sniffing solvents. Perhaps the greatest risk with solvents is that many young children as well as teenagers see this as a cheap way of having a good time. Sadly some die at the first attempt. Don't do it, don't encourage it, and do report it if you know it's going on – you may well save someone's life.

Specs

see also Popularity, Self-Worth

It's hard to understand why people still have a go at others who wear specs. The silly names and insults fly around despite the fact that everyone is all too keen to wear them with tinted lenses in the summer!

Specs do lots of good things. Specs help you see at least as well as people without them – four eyes have got to be better than only two! Specs add interest to the face and another dimension which makes the wearer stand out in a crowd. Specs provide the wearer with something to do when they are feeling nervous, by taking them off and cleaning them. Specs make wearers look brainy and mature.

Wearing specs is nothing to be ashamed of. Pop stars wear them, so do footballers (off the field) and tennis stars. Specs do not change who you are, but they may well make you look a bit more interesting!

Sport

see also Fitness, Football

Sport helps you keep fit. Sport attracts attention to you. Sport is a healthy, fun way to spend your time, and if you're good at it, you can feel really satisfied that you can achieve things too.

Sport can also be a nightmare for those who are not good at it. We've all see the look on the faces of the less able footballers when they are left to last when teams are picked. For some lads sport can be real agony and it's not helped by insults and criticisms from the athletic types around! Sport also encourages a competitiveness which can seem to say 'winning is all that matters' rather than 'it's the taking part that counts'. While winning is important, the suffering of those who do their best but don't win should also be acknowledged.

If you are good at sport, be grateful to God and the people who have helped you develop your skills. If you're not, don't worry – just have a go and do your best. That's the most anyone can fairly ask of you.

Spots

see Cleanliness, Zits

Suffering

see Poverty

Suicide

see also Depression

Suicide is simply when someone kills themself. There are lots of ways that people try this and many attempts at suicide fail. There is an alarming rise in the number of teenagers who attempt and, in many cases, succeed in killing themselves, and lots of stories and research about why this may be the case. Suicide is now the third biggest cause of teenage death behind accidents and illness.

Many young people who attempt suicide say that they didn't really want to die, but they simply couldn't see a way through their feelings. When a suicide attempt leads to death, the lives of all those around the young person – parents, brothers and sisters, wider family, friends, teachers, neighbours – are damaged and changed for life. Many will feel responsible and guilty, and they may never understand what happened and why.

You'll know that there's lots of pressure on you right now, and that pressure can sometimes seem too much. Maybe your body is changing, your emotions and feelings are mixed up, you are being pressured to succeed at home and at school, you've not got a girlfriend. When you're young you may think that these situations will never go away, you'll feel down and depressed about it all, and you think you may never be able to cope with them . . . but you will. God never gives us more than we can manage and is always there to help us get through and see his power through everything. Once you get through a rough patch you start to realise that you can cope and things do get better!

Suicide is never God's plan for anyone. If you're feeling really depressed, get help, talk to anyone who will listen and remember the key truth – God will help you whatever!

Tt

Teachers *see also Exclusion, Homework, School*

Did they land from outer space or are they from a mysterious underground world? Perhaps you see your teachers as a great support and inspiration, and perhaps not. It's more likely that most of them seem to have it in for you and do all they can to wind you up.

You have to go to school and you have to spend time with teachers. Most of them do the job because they care about you and your peers and they want to see you succeed. Many could find easier and better paid jobs where they don't have to look at spots and grease all day! They nag for your homework because they don't want you to get behind, they push you to try harder because they want you to do your best, and they have a go at you when you talk too much because they don't think you've a right to stop others from learning. There are a few nasty teachers around too, but if you're honest, you probably don't see many of them.

The thing to remember about teachers is that they want to help you, and if you've got a problem, it's their job to talk it through. They will inspire you to really succeed if you let them.

TV

see also Certificate 18, Soaps

TV is a great escape. It's good to relax in front of and enjoy some gentle mind-numbing stuff. It can keep us connected with the real world through news and features, and it has great sports coverage. It can help people relax and have a break, and it can even teach new things.

TV is not all bad, but, like the phone, friends and hobbies, it can take over and suck away all your time. If it's on in the house all the time, it's not easy to settle to something else or do your homework while watching the latest episode of The Street! You will know what it's like to sit watching some rubbish for hours before realising what the time is and what you should have been doing.

TV and videos also have things on which are not helpful for you to see. Sex scenes will not help you understand what sex in a loving relationship could mean to you in the future. Violence and horror can mess up your view on life and make you scared and paranoid. Perhaps you could try thinking, 'Would Jesus sit with me and my mates while we watch this?' TV is a tool in your control, so don't let it control you.

Uu

Ugly

see also Popularity, Self-Worth

Who says what is ugly and what is not? You might think that a building is revolting, while someone else will go into raptures about its delicate lines and other such nonsense!

You might think you're ugly at the moment because your brace, spots or grease don't help what you look like. But remember that you're developing into something different, and to some people you're far from ugly. Your mum thinks you're handsome, your grandma looks at your photo every day, and God thinks you're the bee's knees!

It's probably even worse for girls. They can get really hung up on what they look like to you, when you might think they are a picture of heavenly beauty! Don't listen to anyone else when it comes to what's ugly and what's not – just trust your instincts and go for it.

Uni

see also Careers, Decisions, Independence

Over the last 15 years the number of teenagers going to university or college after school has grown massively. It used to be an unusual thing to do, but now in many areas it's the norm.

You might not have to decide yet, and you might not like the idea anyway. Uni keeps you a student and you don't have the freedom to work and earn much. You'll probably end your course in debt. But it does give you a chance to get away, live a bit and take on some of those responsibilities that men do. You could also grow massively in your faith and be able to mix with a huge range of other Christians.

Staying at home gives you a bit of comfort but keeps you tied to the family rules. You may find that there's a course at a local college that is more suited to you, or you want to get out of school and you've got an eye on a job or two.

Whether uni is the place for you or not, it's best to get all the help you can before you start to make plans – and don't forget to ask God to show you what he has in mind for your future!

Vv

Valentine's Day *see also Girlfriends, Love*

Valentine's Day is a bit of a laugh and you shouldn't take it too seriously. It's a bit embarrassing seeing the cards your parents buy for each other, and it's a bit nerve-racking waiting to find out whether you've been sent a Valentine or not!

If you have got a special girl in your life, don't forget to get her something a little bit special – this means more to her than it does to you. And if you find that she's got another Valentine too, don't get upset – just be proud that you have managed to catch a girl that another boy wants too!

Whatever you get or give on Valentine's Day, it's what you are willing to give the rest of the time that matters. Love isn't about one day each February!

Vegetarians *see also Diets, Food*

You may be wondering how anyone could dream of surviving without bacon sandwiches and sausages, or you may be revolted by the thought of eating pigs! Vegetarians are now becoming increasingly common and there's nothing wrong with people living by their convictions by not eating meat. The Bible encourages us to eat well, and says that animals can be used for food, but it's not likely that God will disapprove of someone who chooses to eat fruit and veg instead.

If you are thinking about giving up meat or you've already done so, make sure that you've talked to your parents about it. They will need to make sure that you are eating the right balance of food to make up for what you're not getting in meat. And don't do it just because you want to impress someone. This is a matter of personal conviction and should be thought through properly first.

Videos

see Certificate 18, TV

Virgin

see also Sex

This is more than a brand name for coke, music and railways! It means to be clean, to be pure and to be untouched. It's a good word, not an insult.

A girl who is a virgin has something to be proud of and shouldn't be teased or bullied because of it. A virgin has decided not to get into sex too soon and is probably waiting for her life-partner to come along. She is not going to be used by boys. Likewise, if you are a virgin, you should be really happy about yourself. You do not need to go along with the crowd and do what you feel is wrong inside. You are able to make your own mature decisions and keep one of God's greatest gifts until it really matters. And, finally, don't always believe what your friends say about themselves – many of them have vivid imaginations!

Voice

Your changing voice is something that just has to be endured, no matter how much of a pain it is! Your voice has to break at the same time as your body changes and hair grows, and it's another of those steps which makes you less of a boy and more of a man.

Your voice may change quite suddenly over a few days, or it might drag on over weeks. Inevitably you will find that you start to squeak halfway through a sentence or your voice takes a dip underground when you are trying to make yourself understood. There is nothing at all you can do to stop it happening. Your mates will find it hilarious until it happens to them, and girls will find it hilarious and don't have to go through it – they've got one over on you here!

If you know it's beginning to happen, try to avoid situations where you are expected to say much, particularly at school or church. If you talk a little more slowly than usual and stay calm, it may help, as the voice can go a bit wild when we're excited anyway. And when it's all over you may have developed a really good voice that you like . . . all being well!

Ww

Wants

see also Money, Poverty, Shops

There are things we want and things we need. There are things we really yearn for which we don't really need at all. The sad fact of teenage life, and the whole of life for most of us, is that we will never have everything we want. God already provides us with what we need, which is why we pray for it and thank God for it every time we say the Lord's Prayer. We need somewhere to live, food and clothing. We want more friends, CDs, money, computers, bikes, girlfriends. We may be able to get some of those things, but if we're always wanting more, we will always be frustrated and disappointed. Jesus talked of how God always gives us what we need and therefore we shouldn't bother to waste our time worrying about the other things. If you think about all the things you have right now, you'll find that there are plenty you don't really need anyway.

War

see also Armed Forces

War is often portrayed as being attractive, glamorous and exciting. It involves complex and fascinating hardware including guns, tanks, ships, helicopters and missiles. It can look like fun.

War is about killing people. Whatever the reason a nation enters into a war, be it for the protection of others, self-defence or the desire to take over another country, a war inevitably means that people will die. Some of the people who'll die will be soldiers and others in the Armed Forces, but others will be normal people going about their normal lives. Everyone who dies will be someone's son or daughter, parent or grandparent. War is not nearly as exciting as films make it out to be, and the reality of the injuries and deaths caused can stay deep in the memories of those who fight for the whole of their lives.

War is not always wrong, but it is a bad thing that God doesn't want in his world.

Peace is what we should all be working for and praying for, and it takes guts to want to be peaceful and not aggressive.

Weight

see Diet

Women

see also Girls, Mothers

Men and boys will never fully understand women and girls! They are special and very different from us! Biologically and physically, women are smaller than men, carry more fat and have less muscle. Emotionally, they are often more sensitive, aware of how others feel and more able to express their feelings. There are some myths about women which are probably not true . . . although you may know different! It is said that women talk more than men, that they spend longer in the bathroom and that they change their minds all the time.

Women are not made to be the slaves of men or children. Even in this enlightened age there are still a few situations in the workplace and in society where women are seen as being lesser mortals, probably because they have traditionally taken the leading role in giving up careers to look after children. God made us all equal.

Women, like teenage girls, face times of pain regularly and may become moody and irritable for a few days. When this happens, allow the women in your life a little space and try not to make it worse for them.

Thank God for all the women in your life and remember to treat them properly.

Work

see also Careers, Laziness

There's always work to be done. You may have jobs in the home, homework or work on your bike to finish. But the world of work awaits and now might be a good time to get some practice in.

There are paper rounds, Saturday jobs and other work around for teenage lads. Most of it will not stretch your brain too much and is not very well paid, but it may bring in that little bit extra to buy yourself a few things you want but don't need. Work also gives you a chance to prove yourself and have some time away from your family, which is often quite a good thing!

If you are looking for work, think about it first. Make sure that you will have time to do the job, have a bit of a social life, keep up with church and still get your homework done. Check that the pay is about the same as others get doing the same job – you don't want to be ripped off. And finally make sure that you will be safe and properly equipped for whatever you do.

Worship

see also God, Prayer

This is all about coming into the presence of something great. People worship at football grounds as their heroes run on to the pitch. Others worship at pop concerts.

God calls us to worship him as we remember how fantastic it is that his Son Jesus died for us and lives for us.

Through worship we can really feel God close to us. We can worship through prayers, through silence, through singing, through dance, through clapping and through making music.

Worship is essential if you really want to grow as a Christian. Sometimes worship can seem really tedious and dull, but if you try to get into it with the right attitude, God will speak to you through it. As a younger person you may be able to express your worship more energetically and openly than others do, and that's fine. Worship is only about the relationship between you and God, and that should be your focus.

If you want to know more about worship, talk to your youth leader or church leader, but don't ignore it. As you worship God, he could change your life!

Xx

X-files

see also Evil, Occult

The X-Files is an old TV programme that gives the impression the world is full of strange happenings that can't be explained . . . ask someone old about it! These types of programmes and films make people think twice about the world in which we live and expect to find weird things happening everywhere. People get obsessed with supernatural things and are always looking to find the cause.

No doubt for the Egyptian Pharaoh at the time of Moses there were plenty of unexplained happenings going on, with frogs, locusts, plagues and whatever. But there was an explanation for those – it was the Creator God. Now there are still things that we don't understand, but the only real, powerful supernatural power is God. Don't worry about anything else, just trust him.

Yy

Youth Groups

see also Church, Gangs, Worship

Youth groups are a really useful way to learn about life, about others and about God. A good Christian youth group will have leaders who care enough about teenagers to give up their time and energy to work with you. In a youth group you will have easy access to girls, other friends to get to know and lots of fun to enjoy. There may be social events, trips and holidays. You will have friends to support you when you have problems or when you stand up for your beliefs at school. You will make friendships that may last you all your life. You will also have the opportunity to learn more about God in a way that is relevant and exciting for you.

It's really hard being a teenage Christian on your own, so if you are, try to find others like you and get something going, even if you have to do it yourself.

Zz

Zits

see also Cleanliness

Spots, blotches, blackheads, acne, pimples . . . oh help! These are always likely to appear on your skin just at the wrong time. You wake up on the morning of going to a new school with your face looking like the surface of the moon! You want to draw a new girl into your arms when your chin explodes with great big oozing volcanoes!

The first thing to say about such things is that they don't look nearly as bad to others as they do to you! You know what your face has done because you have studied it in the mirror, but others don't.

The second thing about the zit family is that they pass. As your body is bursting with hormones to make it grow and change, spots explode, but as things calm down and manhood approaches, so most of the spots go away.

The third thing is that you can avoid them or at least keep them from getting worse by doing some simple things. Make sure that you wash your skin as often as you can in clean warm water and an antiseptic wash or mild soap. Eat a balanced diet and try to keep fit. Use creams and lotions as directed on the packet but don't expect miracles. And go to the doctor if it's really bothering you.

Some contact addresses, phone numbers and websites

AIDS	National Aids helpline: (0800) 567123 www.thewellproject.org
Alcohol Abuse	Alcoholics Anonymous (AA), London helpline: (0171) 352 3001. Head Office, PO Box 1, Stonebow House, York YOI 7NJ. (01904) 644026 Alcohol Action Wales, 8th Floor, Brunel House, 2 Fitzlan Rd, Cardiff CF2 1EB www.alcoholics-anonymous.org
Childline	(0800)1111. Freepost 1111, London N1 ORR NSPCC Childline: (0800) 800500 www.ChildLine.co.uk
Christian Holidays and Mission Projects	Scripture Union: 207 – 209 Queensway, Bletchley, Milton Keynes MK2 2EB. Tel: (01908) 856000. Fax: (01908) 856111 www.scriptureunion.org.uk

Crusaders (Crusoe):
2, Romeland Hill, St. Albans, Herts
AL3 4ET

World Horizons, North Dock Centre,
Llanelli Dyfed.
www.worldhorizons.co.uk

Drug Abuse

Lifeline: (90161) 8392054

Re-Solv (Society for Prevention of
Solvent and Volatile Substance Abuse):
30a High St, Stone, Staffs ST15 8AW
www.drugfree.org

Eating Disorders

Youth Helpline: (01603) 765050
Mon – Fri, 4 – 6 pm

The Eating Disorder Association:
First Floor, Wensum House,
103 Prince of Wales Rd, Norwich,
Norfolk NR1 1DW. (01603) 621414

The Anorexia and Bulimia Nervosa
Association, Tottenham Women and
Health Centre Annexe, Tottenham,
London N15 4RK
www.nationaleatingdisorders.org

Giving up Smoking	Smoker's Quitline: Wales: (01222) 0641888 London: (0171) 4873000 ASH (Action for Smoking and Health), 5-11 Mortimer Street, London W1A 4QW www.nhs.uk/gosmokefree
Pregnancy Advice	Care Centre Network: CARE (0800) 0282228 www.pregnancy.org.uk www.christiananswers.net/pregnancy

Nick Harding can be contacted through the publisher's address at the front of the book. He can also be found on Facebook!